The Jade Bust
Short Stories

BY Gregory Anton Chakmak

CONTENTS

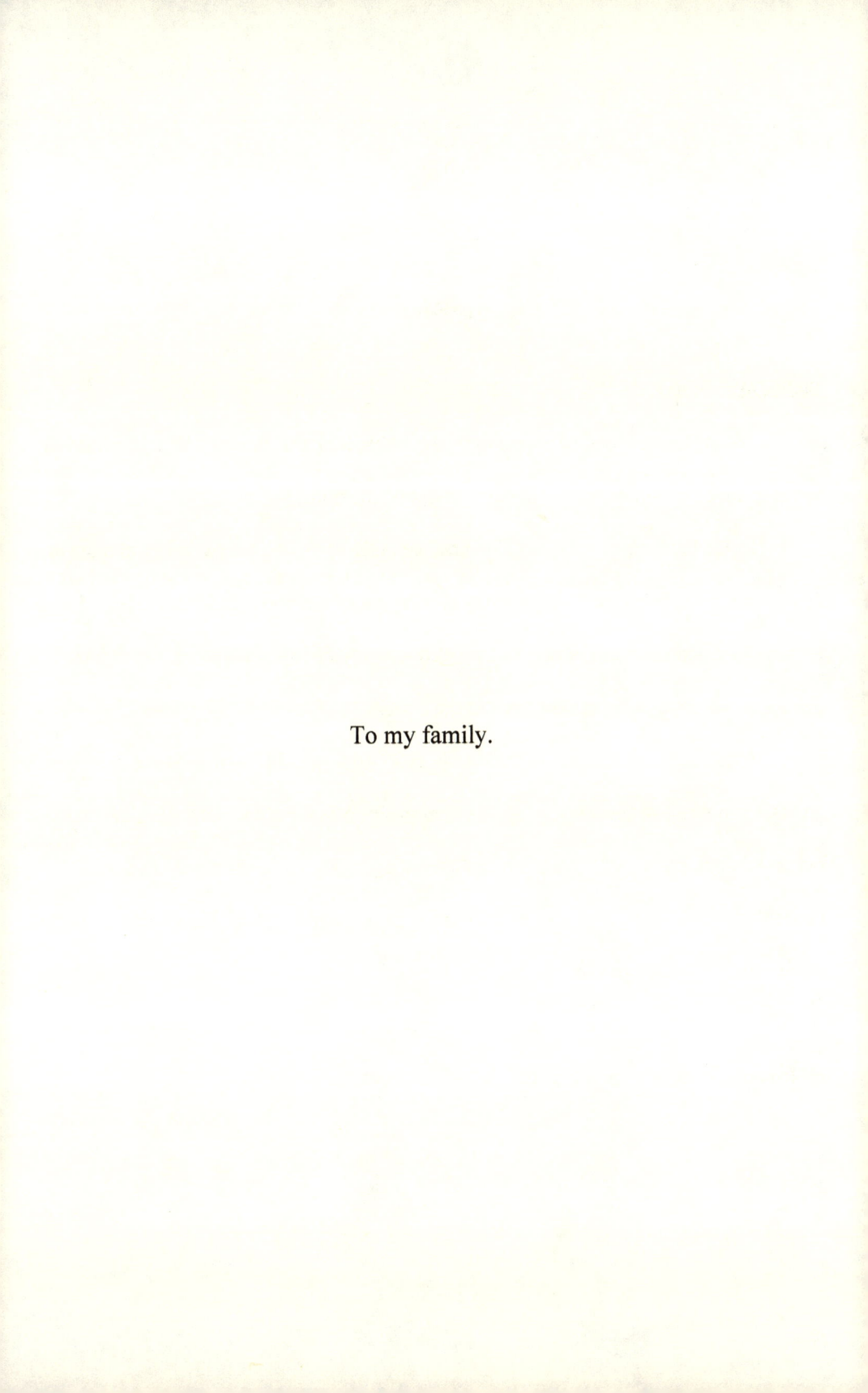

To my family.

The Seven Do

TUESDAY 3:30 PM:

When Ben got home he went to the mailbox, took the mail out, and then hurried to get the door key in the slot. He then, unlocked the door.

Inside he went past the old wood coffee table, throwing his backpack and the mail down, and ran through the kitchen to the laundry room bathroom and went. He had to go for the last fifteen minutes, and it had worked it's way up to a pitch as he was unlocking the door. His Jade backpack dropped to the floor.

After, he made his way to the couch, plopped down, and turned on the TV. Oprah and Batman was just finishing up and Pokemon- Jotto League was next. "Mom" he cried out and no one answered. "Mom" he called out again louder, and no one answered. He probably knew I. He got up and walked to the garage and checked, his Mom's car wasn't there. He walked back to the kitchen, got an ashtray and the long handled range lighter from the cupboard, and walked back to the couch. He fished through his backpack and pulled out a pack of Camel Lights. He took one out and lit it.

It was a fairly sized room, about 25 feet by 12. It had wood paneling on the walls with a beige carpet on the floor and bluish brown couches. They were set up in an "L" shape facing the TV. As the room began filling up with waves of white smoke Ben remembered to open up the sliding glass door. When he opened it, he watched as puffs of air swirled the smoke and drew it outside. He walked over to the coffee table, ashed his cigarette, sat down, and picked up the mail.

The first, was for his Mom. The second was for his Dad, then Dad and Mom, Dad, Sister, and then a Macy's catalogue. He pulled the catalogue out and a letter from behind it fell to the carpet. He put the rest of the mail down and picked it up. It was addressed to a Cornel Tom Maryweather, Ben vaguely remembered a Tom as the previous owner of the house and it looked official, from the Pennsylvania State Insurance Company, but still he decided to open it. Inside there was no letter, just a folded piece of thick paper. He pulled it out and unfolded it along the perforation -

Pay to the order of Tom Maryweather, $6323.00, dated September 23. September 23, was two weeks before, it was Tuesday October 7.

Ben couldn't believe his eyes, he put his cigarette out and walked into his bedroom. As he got into the hallway there was a creaking noise in the house and he heard the garage door humming. In a panic he put the check on his dresser up with his backpack ran to the living room picked up the lighter and the ashtray, dumped it in the trash, wiping and covering the ashes with a discarded paper towel, put them away and finally made a dash for the couch to sit down and look comfortable. His Mom was just walking in, her hands full of groceries, "Benjamin I've spoke to you about this smoking crap."

"Mom." Ben answered in a winy tone, picking up the Macy's cataloge and reading.

"Don't lie to me Benjamin, you've been smoking, and in the house!" she yelled leaning over and staring at him after she had put down the grocery bags.

"Mom, I wasn't smoking." he wined again.

Fuming she said, "You just wait till your dad gets home... now go get the rest of the groceries."

"Fine." Ben said and picked up his backpack and went inside to his room, and the garage.   Apple, tomato, lemons.

WEDNESDAY 12:00 AM:

Ben just couldn't sleep. He was thinking about the check. If he could just cash that check, he'd really be in the money. He could take off that summer, maybe never go back for his last year of school or see his stupid home or parents ever again. He could use that money and get a job, he thought. He wasn't picky either, a factory job or sweeping out a stationary store at first, then he could save more money. He could take that money and go far as he could; New York maybe. But then he thought better of himself, being that New York could be too expensive. Yonkers, Chelsea, Upper East. He'd talked to plenty of bums on the street while giving them change. Some had been to every state in the Union, on a lot less money. He could go by bus or buy a junky car or truck and just go. He thought of Thomas Kinkade somewhere in the middle of America, painting his pictures of light. Then he looked at the clock it was 12:36, he had to get up in less than seven hours. He turned to his clock radio and reset his alarm for 7:35, the latest he figured he could get up and still make it to school. He then fumbled his way to the other side of the bed and got comfortable on his stomach, and forced his eyes shut. School maybe. The crickets were chirping outside. The sounds rang loudly then softly as if someone had recorded them in unison and was tuning the volume control up and then down. He listened and thought of outside, sleeping outside. They were outside, singing all night most every night. It was like a drum, he didn't get to sleep until around 2:00 AM.

9:12AM

Ben was sitting in homeroom. The PE room. The American anthem was playing over the intercom. When it was over he put his head down. A few minutes later he was woken up by the bell to go to English, his next class. That night he went to bed early, before his dad got home.

Thursday 6:02AM

That morning Ben got up early and had a cigarette with the sunrise. He had done his homework and slept early, the sky had turned violet then blue, then I don't why, I don't know you, it was a crisp morning. He went inside to find his father already awake drinking his morning coffee. "Morning Ben." he said.

"Morning Pop." Ben answered getting cereal out of the cupboard and sitting down.

"Ben," his dad started, "as long as your up we need to discuss something." He paused, "Your mom's telling me that you've been smoking and smoking in the house no less."

"Dad" Ben said loudly.

"No Ben listen to me..." His dad also raised his tone.

"I wasn't smoking!" Ben yelled at him right away.

His dad shot back, "Look at you, your sleeping odd hours..." Ben at this point loudly huffed "no Ben, no, you look like a mess, and you stink, you constantly stink of cigarettes, your making a fool of yourself."

"Look at you! Married to the ideal that your idea of the future is the one and only. Kissing up to your bosses when all you're really doing is killing us. Marching into a exchange future that is senseless and misguided, you people drive me crazy." Ben yelled.

"Ben I know your a smart kid but soon you'll find out that ideals are great but they're a two way street, if you want to live by your ideals great, but you can't go around stealing and cheating and lying and say your a man of ideals. You'll come to see that when you go down a road it will take you somewhere, even if you don't want to go. You see, your only cheating yourself, now tell me, were you smoking in the house!"

"I can't take this." Ben said coolly and walked out of the kitchen.

Around 4:00PM

Ben that day didn't go home after school. He was going to stay out late and not go home. He didn't want to face his dad and another fight, or even his mom for that matter. He got it into his mind to go to his girlfriends Jill's house, her mom didn't get home until 5:00PM. She lived in the next town over and went to a different high school. He loved her in his own way, but she was going to collage eventually and they were so young, he knew it would be stupid to think of it as anything. He took the bus and went to her house. When he got there he had a funny feeling. She had a lovely house, small and quaint with blue carpeting and nick-nacks on shelves all around, Pinoicios, wizard hats, unicorns it was a little girlish for Ben's taste but nice all the same. I do not know, he thought maybe he was going to tell her about it, the check and his trip. She had a way of always calling him at the right time and knowing what to say. He knew she liked his spontaneity so he was going to see what she was doing, no matter what. It was around 4:00 when he got to her house. Her car was in the driveway.

Ben walked up to the door and ding-donged, at first she didn't answer, but he could hear the television on loud so he knocked and yelled. "Jill it's me open up!" After a full minute Ben heard footsteps come up to the door and then it opened but just a crack; it was Jill. Unicorns and muskrats and baskets full of dead clay fish.

"Ben what are you doing here?"

"Jill I had a fight with my dad I didn't want to go home."

"Well, you shouldn't have come without calling."

"Oh come on, let me in." and Ben sort of pushed at the door.

"Ben" she yelped and then he heard a boys voice call from the bedroom, "Jill who's that at the door? It's getting cold in here."

Ben's stomach dropped, anger flashed "Who's that, what's going on here."

"Ben its nothing I think you should leave." Jill gave Ben pity me eyes.

Anger welled up in Ben, "What the hell, how could you do this?"

"Ben its nothing." she said again and a tall blond haired boy appeared through the door, out of Jill's room, in his boxer shorts, hair a mess, "Honey, do you need some help with this joker?" She turned and said "Chris it's O..." but before she could finish, Ben, unstable as he was looking for release, pushed open the door and took a swing at that half naked, sexed, son of a bitch. Chris quickly pushed Ben off him, "You son of a bitch, I got a shot gun in the car, I'll kill you." and Chris made a break for his car. "No!, no!" Jill yelled. Ben tackled the half naked boy in the yard and kneed him in the back. He got up to kick him but then Jill ran up in front of him, "Nooo". Chris scrambled up to his car and took out a single barrel shot gun. Jill ran up to him. Ben got one last look at them, Jill in her purple fuzzy robe and that guy in his underwear. He just wanted to cry but he couldn't, there was too much adrenaline, he ran around the corner as fast as he could. Red train lights, stop signs, poles, everywhere poles.

He ran past two bus stops waiting for the bus to appear in the distance. When he caught it he couldn't contain himself, began to well up and tear. He thought a lot of thoughts in that bus, some terrible, namely that there was nothing to keep him in that town anymore; he was leaving that town for sure and that he didn't want to be alone that night. He went home that night and sat quietly watching TV with his parents. At six he watched Star Trek, it always cheered him up.

FRIDAY 6:30PM

Ben arrived at Franks Check Cashing at around 3:45, he had gone straight after school. It was a pale paneled, wood covered, box of a place with a bullet proof glass protecting two cashiers facing the street. On the walls were posters from the government in Spanish and English, and interesting enough, lottery posters everywhere. You'd give ten percent to them, use half your check to buy lottery tickets and take the other half home to your family to buy beer maybe, or pay the rent. Maybe me Ben noticed right away but it was odd to see a young White boy on the premises. They answered his questions all the same. Six black lottery checks.

"I have an insurance settlement check, can I cash it here?"

"How much is the check for?" the lady clerk said.

"About 6000.00 dollars." Ben answered.

"Sure that's fine kid. I need to see the check and your ID."

"That's it?" Ben asked.

"Why?" she said eyeing him.

"No, I was just seeing, I'll be back tomorrow." and then Ben turned.

"Hey kid," she called, "were closed on the weekends." No bring your Mom nothing.

"Great, Thank You." he said and left. He decided he wasn't going back on Monday, they would recognize him. He then went to Carlyle's Magic store and bought the best fake mustache he could find, got some dinner and then went to the arcade.

At the arcade he saw some of his friends but he said nothing. Nothing about Jill or the check. He was waiting for John to come on duty as the change manager. John was some loser that worked at the arcade since he graduated high school, he was 24 now and knew the city pretty good. They talked once in awhile and played pinball together. When John came on Ben went up to talk to him.

"John how's it going?" Ben asked.

"Oh, you know, so so." he answered.

"Any good games coming out soon?" Ben continued.

"Naw, everyone creates the new stuff for three year olds or at least three year old mentalities, for all the advancements in graphics, innovation in video games has gone nowhere." John said.

"I know, I know.- John, I have a question for you, if I want to get a fake ID where would I go?" Ben finally said it.

"Well the easiest place is Lake Park, west of Downtown, in the city. That's where all the migrant workers go to get documentation. How old are you seventeen? I did that when I was your age too. Just ask the people standing suspiciously around and before you know it, you'll be buying for your friends." John finished.

"Thanks John." Ben said.

"Yeah Okay." John answered and they parted ways. Around ten Ben went home. Black chain bars and cool tetherballs.

SATURDAY 8:20AM

When Ben got home the night before his parents were waiting up and pissed off. He had not called and didn't get until late. His mom was worried sick. They had called all his friends including Jill, who had told them she hadn't seen him since earlier that week. Ben told them that he was at the arcade, but they didn't care and they sent him to bed. The next morning while his parents were eating breakfast they had a talk with him.

"Ben we've been thinking and we decided that your going to church with us tomorrow." his mom said.

"Mom, it's not a holiday, it's not anything, and I haven't been to church in years." he wined.

"All the more reason. Were all going to go tomorrow." his dad said.

"You guys, but, fine, OK, but I need to borrow the car today. I haven't seen Jill in a while and I need to go and talk with her." Ben said.

"That's fine son, but only if you can take the car make sure and tell us exactly when your coming back. OK?" his dad quickly acquiesced over his Mom's protests, it was great for Ben.

"Of course Dad, of course, I'm really sorry, I will be more responsible." and then after that everyone was happy.

A few hours later Ben borrowed the car and told them he would be back later at four. Down the street he applied the adhesive to his lip and put on his mustache. Then he took out the map and found the way to Lake Park. On a Saturday, it was about a forty minute drive.

When he arrived at the park he was amazed to see the amount of people out and about. There were people everywhere, shopping, playing ball, walking, picnicking, the city was bustling, it was hard to get a parking space. When he finally did get to the park he started out by taking a walk around the lake. He saw an old black man wearing a T-shirt and old dirty jeans. Ben looked at him, he walked up, "Heroine, heroine, you want heroine." Ben was shocked, Weed, Coke, and Speed were one thing, but Heroine in a park with kids running around, "No, man no, I need an ID." he stated.

"Go over by the lake bridge. How 'bout a dollar" he said and Ben answered no. Then he leaned over as if to scare him and put his hand in the top of his T-shirt. Ben quickly walked away. The man had to be a crack addict.

When Ben got to the bridge he noticed a group of Mexicans suspiciously standing around. He lit a cigarette and walked over and whispered "IDs" two or three of them immediately walked over.

"You want an ID?" one man said.

"Why are you a cop?" Ben quipped. One guy got mad, the others started laughing. Ben felt stupid.

"He's a smart kid. No, I'm not a cop. We make licenses."

"Well I need one. And, if it can, I need it to have my picture and a certain name." Ben said.

"A name, were gonna have to make that special. It cost money you know." the man in charge said.

"How much?" Ben asked.

"Maybe seventy dollars, you know?"

"That's fine." Ben answered.

"OK, give us you picture and the name and come back here in two hours."

"Two hours, what am I going to do for two hours and I don't have a picture." Ben remarked.

"Well we can do a rush job, but it will cost you twenty bucks more, and you can get a picture over at the passport photo shop on twenty third. We'll go over with you."

"No, I can figure it out." Ben said, suppressing a flash of fear.

"OK, come back here with the picture and we'll get you your ID."

Ben went off walking. He found the photo shop and the whole thing went pretty smoothly. He chose to wait two hours he said he didn't have any more money, the guy said come back in an hour anyway. In the mean time he sat and smoked, watched the lake and the fountains. He thought the whole thing was like going to buy a hat or something, convenience and service. He got home well before 4:00 and he didn't go out that night.

SUNDAY 10:30AM

In their Sunday's finest the family went out to church. There they met Elizabeth, Ben's older half sister, she was pregnant with her first child. Her husband Frank, an industrialist ass, was with her. He worked for a loan sharking credit card company and he, above all people always seemed to have advice for Ben. Ben was happy to see his sister, he always admired her and she was beaming when she saw him; things were different around the house since she was gone.

During mass the priest was speaking gibberish about how Christ not only brought the Word to the Masses but how he helped the needy and the poor and especially the morally poor see the light of goodness and bring the richness of faith into their lives changing the world spiritually for ever. They said "Peace be with you." Ben's favorite part about church and then they passed the baskets of the real riches around. Everybody faithfully put money in the baskets reestablishing faith in their hearts. It was all very moving, but stupid.

That night Ben examined the ID and went over what he was going to do in his head. The ID looked OK, but the print was bold and some of the lamination was overdone. He trimmed the edges of the ID and hoped for the best.

MONDAY 1:17PM

In Economics, his fifth period class, he got to thinking and dreaming about Jill. Why such a scumball idiot? Why was it like that? He'd never know. He thought about her naked under that purple robe of hers. He wasn't so mad anymore. He put his head down and dreamed.

3:29PM

The moment was here. He took the bus to Ready Chex, the scummiest hole of a check cashing place he knew of. It was in a shopping center south of his house. Its facade had a big yellow sign, "Checks Cashed". He had his check, his mustache on and his ID in his wallet ready to go. He walked in and got in line. When he walked up to the cashier he said in a deep voice, "I'd like to cash this check."

"ID" the clerk said and Ben took it out. The clerk took the ID and the check and stared at Ben a long time. Ben felt perspiration forming on his forehead, he smiled.

"Hold on." the clerk said and he walked over to the manager sitting down at a desk in the back and talked to him, both were looking directly at Ben, and talking.

"Your a mess." Ben heard ring out in his father's voice, "Your making a fool of yourself."

The man came back, "Do you have any other forms of ID?"

"No, that's why I came here." Ben quickly remarked and the man went back to the desk and talked. They looked at Ben again and then the ID. "When you go down a road it's going to take you somewhere, maybe me." he heard his dad's voice again. The clerk, looking at Ben, walked past to Ben's left, and started to make a phone call. Ben watched carefully. The man was now talking, he had the check in his hand. A bead of perspiration dripped from Ben's forehead. There was a deep drum roll drumming in his head as he watched it splash on the ground. "Christ brought the richness of virtue into the poor men's lives." he heard once again. The cashier looked suspiciously at Ben, as he was tapping the check on the counter. He dropped the check... "He's made me," Ben thought, "He's on the phone with the police!" As the man was picking up the check Ben turned and quickly walked out of the business. He was muttering under his breath, "This life's not for me; it's not me; never again; I got to pay attention to what I want, I've hit rock bottom..." he began to run. He caught the bus right away. Inside the cashier just got word the check was good and was ready to tell Mr. Maryweather the money had been cleared.

JOHN JOSEPH

John Joseph was a decent but good boy, but at the time of this story, he was getting more and more distant and distracted. His mother, at her coffee clutch on Saturdays, was saying things like, "He was such a happy boy, I don't know what's happening to him, now he just sits and gazes off into space. He's only nine and I already don't know what to do."

There was nothing really wrong with her boy, he was just truly infatuated with staring off into space. You see, whenever John would stand, turn quickly, get overly excited, or even get up out of bed he would be thrust into total blackness. He then would watch as the blackness evaporated and the light from the room slowly reentered his field of vision. Quite often, John would find himself comically, just standing there starring, jumping to conclusions, trying to keep his balance and then losing himself in the strangeness of the whole affair.

He wasn't worried about his condition. He watched the news, and from what he gathered, it was caused by low blood pressure, which he knew was healthy. He knew he didn't have to worry about heart disease, hypertension (just being too stressed out) or a bunch of other problems; of course he didn't know that as he was a only a simple boy and he didn't have to worry about those problems, or even his health.

One day when walking home from school he heard a terrible crash. It was behind him and he quickly turned to see, unfortunately everything went black. Unable to move he stared fixatedly. He heard a man getting out of his car, and then two men arguing. There was yelling, John at this point laughed to himself because of losing his balance and it seemed silly, then a window shattered and things got even more serious. John's eyes began to tingle, it was going to be over soon. There was a shot, and then some cursing and right as John's field of vision returned the culprit was rounding the corner and speeding off. John saw nothing, he knew nothing, but he ran over to the smashed car anyway. A man lay on the ground dying. He took hold of John's hand and pulled him close and with his last bits of strength moved his hand to John's shoulder and said, "You kid, you I saw you looking strait at us, go tell the police, call 911, go tell them my assassin, remember me." and he fell limp. John fell limp too, crying he ran to the nearest house, he told the woman, "Call 911!" and told her what happened. She called and within twenty minutes John was in a cold, light blue room with a big wooden table, at the police station.

A balding man wearing a blue suit came into the room, "Your parents are on their way John. How do you feel?"

"Okay I guess." John answered.

"Can you tell me what happened today?" the policeman said.

"I don't know, I didn't see anything!" John cried.

"You said you heard a crash and turned. What did you see!" ordered the policeman.

"I, I didn't see them. Its just my way, no, I know" John said frightened. Frustrated the policeman left the boy alone. They continued periodically question him until his parents got there. They found their boy distraught and the police worried about their boy, "That man was a mob boss. Your son witnessed this horrific deed and he still may be able to help us find the assassin. We think he should talk to a psychologist. It will help him remember and get through this." John's parents were shocked and to them a psychologist sounded like a good idea; they sent in the psychologist. He was a short bald man with a big old nose, wearing a blue suit, everyone it seemed was wearing a blue suit, "John, that's your name right?" he said in a benevolent but maliciously condescending voice.

"My name is John Joseph, but I don't know!" John answered faithfully.

"John what happened to you when you were walking home from school today, do you mind telling me?"

John told him the story of what had happened, how the man had talked to him and then ended with, "I didn't see anything." The psychologist wrote in his folder and when he finished writing he said, "Thank you very much John. It was very good of you to talk to me." Later he informed the police and John's parents, in a very serious meeting, that John had been terribly traumatized and was suffering from schizophrenic delusional amnesia and would need one on one counseling for many years to come to resolve his issues.

That night John's parents had a talk with him, "John, how did you like that nice man you talked to today."

They seemed very worried, so John answered the way he thought they wanted, "They were all very nice."

"How would you like to talk to that last man each and every week. He's a doctor and he can help you." they said lovingly.

"No, no more questions Mom. No more. Don't make me. Please. I don't like any of them!" John cried, but his manner, in light of what the doctor said, only worried them more.

"It'll be okay honey, you'll see; don't cry." his mom said consoling him.

That same night, in another part of town, Lucy Fingers was talking to her partner and husband, Edward Delabonte or Lucky Eddy.

"Eddy, my sources say the kid saw everything, he was staring right at us." Lucy said.

"You were sitting in the car the whole time, you didn't see him. How could he have seen us. Don't worry." replied Eddy.

"I am worried. I'm telling you my information is good." said Lucy.

"I'm not killing no kid, Lucy-- got it!" Eddy asserted.

"Were going away then Eddy, cause they got our pictures and the kid 'ell finger us-- got it. We'll be going away."

"All right, all right, G-d damb it. I'll go down there and see the kid. See what I can find out."

"You better Eddy, cause I ain't going away."

"All right baby, now settle down. I'll take care of it." Eddy said inwardly complaining about her dumb sparkly purple colored lipstick.

The next morning Eddy waited at John's school. He had a picture of John taken outside of the police station. He saw John arrive at around 7:45AM. John looked strait at him and didn't react, it was a good sign. He saw John walked to school by himself, he figured both his parents probably work, "He's probably a latch key kid. His dad a Mercury Mountaineer." Eddy thought and he felt sorry for him.

That afternoon Eddy followed John away from school, he went ahead of him and turned on Brookhearst, parked his car and slowly walked to the main street. The kid walked right past the murder scene, it was a bad sign but good for do. Eddy walked behind John and then caught up to him.

"Nice day huh?" Eddy said.

"I'm not supposed to talk to strangers." John answered.

"I'm not a stranger, I live back there over on Brookhearst, I walk this way every day. I see you sometimes, don't you recognize me?" Eddy asked. John looked at the man walking next to him for a long time. He had dark hair, balding in the corners making two peninsulas of skin, he had a small face and pleasant features. He was wearing an Adidas jump suit puma high tops and his top shirts shined in the sun. He looked sort of familiar. Eddy didn't like the kid's silence and put his hand in his pocket and held on to his slapjack tight, he thought of exactly where his revolver was strapped behind his pants, but he wasn't nervous, the calm of determination had overcome his being and he was ready to do what he had to do.

"I'm sorry sir. I guess I keep to myself a lot." John said.

"You know, I heard you saw that horrible killing right back over there the other day."

John felt strangely relaxed in a racially kind, kind of way, "It's weird, but when I turned around, the other day I just saw nothing."

"Like when you get up too fast and see nothing, you mean?"

"Yeah,… that happens to you too." the man made John happy.

Eddy let out a laugh, "That happens to everybody kid, you don't worry about it."

"You really think it's Okay?" John asked.

"You'll be fine kid,… just don't do" there was a pause then Eddy continued, "Well, this is where I turn, I'll see you tomorrow."

"Bye Mister." John said and they parted ways.

The police never did catch up with Eddy or Lucy. And John, never did see any of them again, and after four years of intensive therapy is said to be getting better.

JOHNNY AND DAVID

"No bro you only got five minutes to get away. I've seen plenty of those chases on TV, five minutes that's all you got." Johnny said.

"And then what?" David replied taking a long sip of his whiskey.

"Then bro, you've got ten cops on your ass- helicopters, the news, the whole nine yards," Johnny paused taking a sip of his beer, "with all that shit on your tail you ain't got no chance to get away."

"Come on, lets say you jet into the trees and take off running, plenty have got away that way." David said.

"Man, you got the pigs in the sky," Johnny took another sip from his beer, " infrared, heat sensors, upright citizens, the ironwork front door, kind of crowd, man they got everything going their way. And anyway once you dump your car they'll find it and then they got you that way. I tell you if you ain't free and clear in less than five minutes you might as well give yourself up and avoid that whole circus."

"Your probably right Johnny." David said, "But I don't know. Only a g-d dambed fool would lead anybody on a four hour chase."

"Now you see it my way, either your gonna get away or your not." Johnny in triumph leaned back on his couch, he had his beer in his left hand. With his right he picked up the TV controller and was about to turn on the TV when David broke in, "I've got to go do an errand bro, wanna come?" Johnny put down the TV changer cigarette burned and picked up the half smoked pipe on the coffee table and took a hit, "This shit?" he said.

"I know it's dirty, but there is this kid in Granada Hills that's been buying like there's no tomorrow and it's all my friends got right now bro." David replied.

"Cool, lets go." Johnny said.

"Lets take your car, I brought my bike." David asserted. Johnny grabbed his keys and they were off.

Johnny was a reddish blonde haired medium build young man. He had worked out a little, but he had never really gotten into the whole steroid scene, he was twenty-one and lived at home in a separate room from the house. He was a troubled young boy and now that he had a job, in the parts department of a car dealership, his mom didn't bother him much anymore.

David had another story, he was real screw up, but he was a friend of Johnny's. He was Korean, had an oval face with a pointy chin that would stick out. David ended up getting into Heroin in high school, spent a lot of his time in drug dens and ended up dropping out of high school. He was twenty-four and had been clean (of at least the hard stuff) for a year. Even though he was naturally of a medium build, he seemed diminished physically and mentally from years of hard playing and parting. He always seemed to have money, which was a good thing, and had put on some weight in last few months giving him a little beer belly.

On the way to Granada Hills David got on his cell, "Scott...yea, I'm coming up right now, don't go jumping to conclusions. Meet me at the park... yeah on the corner. See ya, bye." David hung up. They drove up to O'Hara park and David sold that naive of a kid a dime bag for fifty, it was easy money. On the way back to Johnny's it was quiet and Johnny broke the silence, "In the grand scheme of things we don't amount to much."

"Why you have to go and say something depressing like that?" David replied.

"No really, you want to go on selling dime bags to boys your whole life? I'm working my lame job, there's nothing to it. There's no point. One of these days were gonna get serious and then what's going to happen... Jail?" Johnny remarked.

"Bro, jail just a lot of time to think about things- were all in jail, we just don't know it. The only time I really experience freedom is on my bike." David said.

"Hey is that thing legal?" Johnny asked.

"You know me better than that." David said with a smile and then continued, "You see, when you open up the throttle and your easily going one hundred and twenty. Your at the mercy of the road, the elements and the other drivers, and only when you give in to it, the world around you- and you trust- and you know- and your going, only then are you truly free."

"I've ridden bikes before, and I don't get what your saying." Johnny said.

"Bro, when you get on a real bike, you'll understand... only when everything owns you and you still do it are you free. Freedom is acceptance." David said.

"I've never heard you talk like this before, David." Johnny said.

"I guess I'm getting older." David replied.

"It happens." Johnny said.

"And don't you forget." David joked and they both laughed.

"Bro," David said, "why do they call when a truck hauls a load, shipping? What does shipping have to do with a truck?" David said then continued, "J.B. Hunt is that huntsman do?." Johnny stayed silent, nothing to say.

When they got to Johnny's house David had to take off. "See you bro." he said and he left. Johnny went inside finished the bowl of his pipe and watched some TV. That night he thought about what David said and then he was asleep.

The next morning he gave David a call. He told him he had been thinking about what he said and had decided to get a motorcycle of his own. He asked David to come over so he could try his bike out. David was okay and said he'd come over in the afternoon. Exited and anxious Johnny started drinking early and watched basketball on TV.

Around noon David arrived, "So your finally going to do it." David said.

"Yeah, I'm going to give it a try." Johnny answered.

"Listen bro, don't just try it, take it down to the beach. Cruise it around, your gonna be hooked. Don't worry about it, gimme your keys and we'll meet later, all right?" David said.

"All right, I'll meet you here around seven and we'll go out." Johnny said.

"All right bro just be cool, you think if they pull me over in your car I should pull over?." David said.

"Hey you don't worry about me, I'm just going to take yours out for a little while." Johnny replied.

"Fine I'll see you around seven." David took Johnny's keys and rushed off. He was late. He was buying a pound and a half of marijuana from some Mexicans in East LA. That new kid in Granada Hills was just I didn't know enough to think he could become a big time dealer and buy a large amount. David had been reeling him in for four months and the time was just right. When he got to East LA it was about 1:00pm. He parked Johnny's car and went up into his connection's Elias' apartment. As usual he was smoking dope with his friends or at least that's what David thought at first. "Pues, David sit down." Elias said after opening the door. David sat down. "Make yourself a drink and kick back." David got up, poured himself a Crown Royal and sat back down. The guys in the apartment began whispering in Spanish, David only made out a little of it. "No he's cool." Elias said, "Your cool right David."

"What's going on?" David replied.

"Nothing," Elias said, "my vatos apartment, just down the street, got busted last night. We just want to know what's going on."

"Elias," David said, "if your not cool with this lets do it on another day."

"No, ese sit down, relax it's the NBA finals you know." Elias said.

"Ya I see." David said. Elias and his friends laughed amongst themselves and they all sat and watched the game.

Meanwhile Johnny was looking over the bike. He started it then shut it down. He took the engine cover off and examined the mechanics of the machine. Finally after about an hour he took it out for a test drive. Slowly he came out of first and he was cruising along, as he went through the gears he could feel the wind on his face, and the floor rushing past him. He thought he was slowly realizing what David was taking about and he decided to let it go on the freeway. Just to see, he thought. He had ridden dirt bikes before, when he was young with his uncle, and his old confidence on the horse was coming back.

As he got on the freeway Johnny took it easy at first getting the feel of the bike. He seemed to be going a comfortable speed, but when he looked down at the speedometer he was going eighty-five. The fact that the bike still had tons of power to spare brought on an indescribable excitement and joy to him. Unleashing this monster was at his finger tips, but something held him back, he didn't gun it just cruised comfortably along, marveling at the power.

Then it happened. As he was nearing the 405 and 101 interchange a siren rang behind him. He looked in his mirrors and there was a black and white behind him. His heart fell into his stomach. He wasn't too drunk he was sure of that, but the bike, he knew David, he knew that that guy had to have something shady with the motorcycle. He was going to jail- the bike was no way legal. The siren rang again, he turned around and looked quickly and began to pull over. The cop rang the siren again, braaamp, like he didn't know he was slowing down and pulling over. That asshole, Johnny thought, if he had any idea what was going on. Then he rang it again, what does he want me to do? Kill, myself? Still Johnny made his way over. And then the ultimate humiliation, the cop blared over his bullhorn, "Pull over, pull over in the shoulder before the freeway. Johnny obeyed. And then they came to a safe and complete stop. Johnny looked at his watch, I'm going to jail, he thought, my job, my life. He looked at his watch again, five minutes. In an instant of certainty he gunned the bike and was off like lightning onto the 101.

It was like a tiger being let out of his cage, within 9 seconds he was hitting 110 weaving in and out of traffic. He knew he had to get off the freeway and fast and get up into the mountains, he had five minutes, or even less.

An exit came up fast and went right by, "The next one for sure." he thought, and he went over to the shoulder and let it loose. A few seconds later he was off the freeway. He didn't hear any sirens, but knew they had to be on his tail. He gunned it onto the street, but their was traffic up ahead he swung out to the shoulder of the wrong side of the street and blew though a long yellow light. He was flying now, traffic from the other direction were blaring their horns and swerving to get out of the way. With each on coming car there was a rush of adrenaline raising him up and then letting him down as he passed by. And then he saw it Ventura Canyon, he zoomed right by it, it would take him into the mountains and complicated roads and places to hide. He slammed on the brakes, popped the clutch using all his weight so the bike wouldn't flip over and turned the bike around. He got right into the left hand turning lane and zoomed left. He was on his way to freedom.

A minute later and after a maze of streets he began to calm down. He looked at his watch three minutes and thirty seconds, he saw a dirt road into a wooded area off the mountain road. He followed it to a clump of old oaks that probably were there because of California environmental laws which was a good thing and Johnny said a prayer of thanks to the tree huggers. He put the bike down and began to cover it with leaves and acorns. He didn't know what he was doing and he hadn't, through all of the chase. Their was a small stream flowing a little ways away, he climbed down to it and washed his face. He looked at his watch five minutes and ten seconds. He took a rest. Later he climbed back to the bike, sat under the cover of the trees and waited to hear the helicopters, nothing, he was safe. He stayed there over two hours- he got away.

David was sitting and watching the game with Elias and his buddies. It was a semi-final game and it was a run away. A few minutes into the fourth quarter Elias said, "Fuck this, it's over."

"Your ready?" David said and they went down stairs to the parking port. Elias popped the trunk of his Mercury and showed David the stuff. David said, "Okay let me go and get my car." He went out to his car and brought it around to Elias'. He got out and reached in his pocket to get out the money when cops like a swarm of bees flew out from ever corner, guns drawn. The Mexicans jumped in their car and took off. David jumped in his and punched it, swerving through the police officers, he made out to the street. He jetted down Soto to Olympic. He knew he couldn't get on the 10 and turned down Crenshaw. There was a line of police behind him and nowhere to go. After exactly five minutes, and thoughts of getting on the 110, he gave himself up.

Johnny satisfied there were no more helicopters after him set back out on to the road. He drove slowly, relishing the sun and the wind and the road and his freedom, he was free. He didn't notice in front of him a car was making a left turn inside one of the many curves on that old canyon road. When Johnny realized what was happening he swerved out of the way. On the edge of the road was a fallen tree branch, he hit it and the bike flipped throwing him. Johnny laid the horse down with an almost slow motion like grace. As he hit the ground his head got caught between his body and the floor. His head was almost severed. It hurt, it was almost deadly.

The Mexicans made the five, and six o'clock news, with a three hour, high and slow speed chase.   The monkey found their way.

The Rousseau's Story

Dear Reader,

There is nothing so strange in this world that can't happen to you. I myself am not a risk taker. I don't play the lottery unless, of course for me, it gets up to seventy five million. I don't really go out, at least not lately, except for weddings and funerals. I don't drink. And I even usually don't say the things that are on my mind. But I do believe that when ever you can, you should help other people, and stay true to your character, even if it means being a bit nosey, and that's what got me into the trouble I'm about to relate.

It wasn't more than two weeks ago, when I was coming home from work. That day didn't go well for me, as I found out that our company (which I won't mention here) was filed with a class action suit alleging, how shall I say it, corporate avarice, board improprieties, and greed. The day was a mess and I was glad to be getting home. I was on the second half of my drive, marked by a sweeping s-curve, with no lights, where I step on it a little and lean into the turns; my daily excursion into my car's grip, balance, handling, strife, and red lights, braking. It's a fairly industrial and deserted strip of road curving around the outside of the Mission Airport; a local airport used mostly for private planes. You could imagine my surprise when around the end of the "S" there was a high dressed girl parked more than half way in the number one lane with her hazards on, trunk and hood open. Fortunately, I was able to comb the brake and got by her OKay. She was a tall black woman in her late thirties in a beautiful black dress with a broad swatch of brown sequence on it. She looked out of place, of course because, there is nothing so formal to do in that part of town. A little further up, where it was safe to pull over, I came to a complete stop where I turned on my hazard lights. A little shaken, but worried about the woman out in the road like that. I took a deep breath, got out of my car, put on my jacket, got a few flares and an umbrella out of my trunk and made my way over to her white Ford Probe. She was standing behind her hatch back, but noticed me and walked to the front of her car.

"You having trouble?" I asked.

She gave me a big smile, "Right on, thank you very much for pulling over."

I went on, "Well, I had these in my trunk. You know your practically out in the middle of the street, it's really very dangerous."

"Oh. I was driving along and I just lost control of my car. My battery light came on and that was it, I was stuck here."

"I got a cell phone, do you want me to call AAA?"

"Sweet of you, but you see I'm late for a very important occasion. I don't have time for AAA, I need to get this done, now." She urged.

"Have you tried it since it stalled?"

"No, I was about to, I was checking the battery connections first."

"You sound like you know more about cars than I do. Give it a try and I'll set these flares."

As I walked around her car I noticed her passenger side front tire was flat. She tried the engine and it started. She began to cheer with joy.

I walked over to the passenger side door looked in and said, raising my voice because she was revving the engine, "I'm sorry to tell you this but you got another problem; your tire over here is flat."

She looked at me, there was a violence to her face that came naturally to her, but was exasperated by her necessity to get going. It softened as she comprehended what I said. "What? Really?" she said.

"I'm not lying to you. You have a flat out here. You got a spare?" A little dejected she turned off the engine.

"I think so,"

"Well, you better get it out."

"Thank you sir." she said perking up, understanding that I was going to help. I felt a warmness in my heart, probably from the selfish satisfaction that I was doing a good deed. We walked around to the back of her car and I reached in to lift a picture in her trunk hatchback so I could get the particle board up and get at her spare. What happened next was almost comical.

Angrily she said, "No, I'll get it" and she pushed me out of her way with her high rear end. The sequence of her dress stuck, for a second, on my slacks. The picture in her hatchback was covered with a blanket. It was big for her trunk so it was propped up sideways. Carefully she lifted the picture with one hand and then scratched at the carpeting of her car with the other. This went on for almost a minute, then when she finally got hold of the particle board, she mistakenly let go of the picture and it banged its way back into place. She then was forced to drop the trunk covering and made sure the picture didn't get damaged. I just stood there annoyed, holding my umbrella; it was beginning to drizzle.

I watched her labor over and over again. Finally, on the fifth try it happened; she had the painting on a steep incline wedged between the roof of her car, the hatchback and the carpeting flooring of her trunk hatchback and the carpeting flooring slipped and she lost control of the painting completely. She cried "S--t", The picture screamed down through her car like a child riding a steep slide, making a terrible thudding noise as it hit the backs of her front seats. She dropped the cover again. The blanket covering it had slid off the painting. She dragged it up close to examine it. I recognized it immediately. It was the Rousseau from the collection at the Norton Simon Museum. Every time I'm at the museum I wallow over it. Its vibrant greens, the leaves, the trees, and that damn monkey holding a pear or an orange or some kind of tropical fruit, or mango maybe. It was its focal point. Seeing it there in front of me I was taken in, unconsciously I didn't know, I ran my hand and my fingers lightly over the paintings surface and looked at its strokes.

"Hey!" she yelled. I pulled my hand away and with fright looked at her, I thought nothing true. There had been nothing in the papers about the painting being lost, sold or even stolen; I just looked and thought.

"Sorry, it's a long story, you should just forget it." she said.

My heart began to race, what did she mean I should forget it? She made me wonder: was this the real painting?, I don't know where it came from, but finally I just said it, "No, I've got time. I'd like to know the story behind this painting."

"You recognize it?"

"Yes. It's the Rousseau, from the Norton Simon."

"Are you going to change my tire?"

"Maybe two."

Tepid but needing me and wanting to get going, she continued, "Well take out the spare, and I'll tell you the story."

"Fine, thank you" I said handing her my umbrella, she put it over us. The rain began falling a little bit harder. I took out the spare and her tire iron and her jack and got to work. She began her story:

"It was sixteen years ago when Hal B--------, the news castor, spent a fortune on a Van Gogh painting. He took the painting, with all his reason and reasons, and straight away hung it in his bedroom. It was a really wild work, a hillside with bushes and flowers and weeds going everywhere. Hal everyday, would just look at the painting and think I think of the true nature of art and viewer and the way, the way of life verses being.

Before and after work, he would follow the curves of every hue and bold stroke. He would just let go in blame, love, want and envy. He would just touch it, the way you did with that Rousseau. And sometimes, at first, he would take a dry brush and go over the lines faster and faster. Then later like in a trance he would just stare at it, go straight to his bedroom and stare at it, sometimes touch it. Every night and every day it was the same thing: home, work, home, painting. He was obsessed.

He stopped seeing his friends on a regular basis. Even his wife eventually began to get jealous. He stopped performing. He would say not here honey lets go downstairs, lets go to the kitchen, he would say lets go anywhere but in the bedroom. But, he never let it get in the way of his work, he didn't let go, he was a real pro.

His wife, you see, was caught in a strange multi-angled spiral. She would ask, why?, but he couldn't explain. He would try, say things about possession, passion, wonder, envy, and understanding, fault, the truth and the true nature of art, but it made no sense to anyone but me. The painting was his only hobby and all of his spare time. Like his work, it was taking over. Eventually, his wife laid it on the line, 'I don't know what you are, or will become, I don't know what your becoming' she said, 'your passion for this has become a pit and we're falling deeper. I don't know what else to do, you have to get rid of that painting.' He did, like you, he looked at her and said absolutely nothing. Enraged, she stormed from the room.

A few weeks later Hal called her at her sisters house. He left a message that he loved her and she should come to the house the day after the next day, Saturday. When she got there there were a few of their closest friends already there mingling and drinking. They were happy to see her. A few more were to arrive.

The mood was somber. Everyone in some way or another had heard the story and was worried. Eventually he greeted his guests. There was a distracted distance in his eye, but he explained everything was alright and he just wanted everybody to go to the garage so he could show them something. The whole garage was painted black. There were bright halogen lights on, and in the back was the painting.

It stood on a stand. An easel of some kind he had made with wood and C-clamps. Everyone in the room was tense. Had he lost it? The painting was there, Hal was there, no one knew what he would do. He walked in front of them, not saying a word. Saying the guests were uncomfortable, would be putting it lightly. He made like he was going to say something, but then, he just exploded. The destruction of our world. It was like he wanted Saint John's head on a platter. Violently he began to pound the painting with his fists. It took some time, but he broke its frame and then he began tearing at it. Finally he took a hammer to it and bashed it When it flew to the ground he jumped and stomped on it. His producer from the show joined in jumping and stomping. The guests began cheering and joining in, ripping tearing at it. Yelling "For me and my eye." We had all done our deepest, guilty desire. There was fear, blood thirst, sexual tension, hate, dislike and a kind of vainglory in the air. The scene went on for an hour or more. It was like some Middle East demonstration against the society we're are and becoming. It was nothing like you ever experienced. I was there. I was his personal assistant.

Eventually, word got out in the entertainment industry, its a legend now. And soon enough, everybody wanted to experience it for themselves. The buzz built and built and finally the whole thing was staged again six years later with the Chagal stolen from the Chicago Institute of Art. It was the biggest little secret in Hollywood; and now, Hal destroyed his Van Gogh sixteen years ago to the day."

As she finished her story, I was finishing up on her lug nuts. "That's quite a story." I said, "Do you mean to say that tonight this painting is... going too?"

"Yeah." she answered mischievously proud.

I was shocked and bewildered and wondered why did she tell me the story? I knew I could never keep this secret. I was dying to ask her how she got the painting in the first place, was it stolen?, and also I wanted to know where and why she was going, but I said nothing. Some time went by in silence. I put the tire in her trunk taking a last look at the painting. She looked at me and said, "So you want to go?"

I was tempted, but I know enough by now to show restraint, "No, I do not know" I answered. I figured nothing could have toped that story of hers anyway. She looked at me jaw dropped. And then I continued, "I guess I'll be there in spirit." She then through me for a loop, "I hope you know your sworn to secrecy." in earnest, I laughed, she was looking at me smiling . Then took my umbrella and left. I never got her name, she never got mine, but I did wonder, and spent many sleepless nights afterward.

Anyway that was my trouble, to tell the Rousseau's story or not. It took me awhile, but I don't know, I've since forgave myself for not going. I did the better, the right thing. As Ben Franklin once said, "Three may keep a secret, if two of them are dead," but the truth is, I think the best secrets *are* the ones that are kept, so keep this one.

So long, and goodbye.

To the Editor of the Daily; Life and Style column.

THE POKER CONSPIRASY

Dear Joseph,

It's been hot, hot and humid. Here where they're believable to me. They're telling me it wasn't always like that in Los Angeles. The old timers I greet tell me twenty years ago, before the legislation requiring hydrogen cars, it was dry here. A virtual paradise, they say.

I know what your thinking, it's not the car companies fault. Well it's not just you guys in Detroit either, the news has got all kinds of reasons for what's going on. They say refrigerators in China alongside the combustion engines still operating all over the globe are to blame. In fact it seems they make up new things nightly on the news- next they'll say it's because we drink too much coffee, which of course affects how we fart! Who knows? They have made us believe everything from the government's honest, to everything must change, till forward motion rather than circular is the truth.

Take for instance what happened to me at this club "insomnia" which I go to and have drinks in the evenings when I can't sleep. I've been going there for almost the whole two years I have been here. They never really had any business (which is the typical for clubs out here) so they began last fall to remodel, embrace new technology, embrace change, as they say. They built a private room in back and lined the walls with Spanish tile and put in red velvet couches, they painted the place all dark yellow and began to play party music very loudly. Well they're business exploded. There was barely any place to sit in the club and the back room only got the most distinguished of customers. It is really a fashionable place to be and in the last few months I've been going more and more.

Last week I was sitting at the bar listening to the hula bulla of all the people at the club. Soon I was bored and decided to go. As I was leaving, Jacob the two hundred and fifty pound bouncer grabbed me by the right arm. He swung me around and a man next to him in a fitted gray suit, younger than me, in his twenties pointed at me and said, "Yeah, he's the guy. He's the dude." Furious I demanded to know what the problem was all about. Jacob, the bouncer, not recognizing me, dragged me all the way to the back room, which was gloriously appointed with gilded moldings and Carrera marble floor, above which the bottom half of the walls had a green granite which led into a kind of red corduroy wall paper. There were statues of cherubs and winged angels throughout the room and in the center was a card table, a roulette wheel and a craps table. As we burst in the craps game stopped cold and the men seated at the card table all turned around and looked. A man with red hair stood up and spoke, "You dirty cheat. What did you think you could bet to the ceiling and just walk out of here?" Confused I said, "What are you people talking about. I demand to know right now!" I put my foot down. The men at the table laughed, "Albert sit down, you old thief, we got business to take care of." A man in a black suit came out of an office in back, he had a pad of paper. They forced me to sit down at the table, the craps game continued. The man in the black suit came up to me and said, "I'm sorry to do this to you, but as we all know that was quite a hand." The men at the table laughed, frustrated I bit my lip and then he continued, "Raise the ante to open, 12,000 on the flop, John over here checks on the turn you check raise him again, honestly Albert with nothing but a strait draw, why did you do?"

"You have confused me sir, I'm not Albert I'm Jack, Jack Coufian." The men started laughing again- "Coufian!"

"Sirs, I'm telling you the truth!" I did know, I said trying to make them understand.

"Ah don't be a wise guy." the Italian looking guy said, "When you asked to get up and go to the bathroom we should have known you were full of it. All said you owe 52,000 dollars, pay up."

That when I didn't know, I stood up, "52,000 dollars are you people insane?"

"Your the insane one Albert, you had nothing but a strait draw, you couldn't get a strait for your momma's wedding ring, now it's time to pay the piper." A man seated at the table said in a horrible voice.

I simply continued, "I'm framed! My name's Jack I tell you, the situation here is uncanny." I took out my wallet and showed the men my ID, desperate I showed them pictures of my family. They all still just laughed, but Mr. Black Suit got very serious. Nervous I looked around and then bolted for the gilt covered door.

"No way, Albert!" Jacob said and caught me by the leg and I fell to the ground. He picked me up and shoved me against the wall. Joseph I can honestly tell you I was afraid for my life. I saw you and your kids in my mind and I prayed as Jacob dragged me past the craps table. Everybody was cursing all sorts of curses and I distinctly remember the shooter at the table rolling a two and a one. I was being taken to the office and my eyes were beginning to well up, I was ready to beg for my life yell bamboo, bloody murder, what ever it took when a boy burst into the room. He walked over to the table and Jacob stopped to listen, "I had Albert on the freeway until the four level, I got on the 110, he must have got on the 101, but we'll get him, I promise you Mr. Carletti." Jacob picked me up, "We got him right here." he said in his rough big voice. "You kidding me?" the boy said, "That's Jack, he's a regular here." That's when I recognized the boy as Mike a bright young waiter/ bus boy at the club. Jacob let go of me dumbfounded. My knees were too weak to stand, so I fell on the ground. The ground was cold and awful, I savored the feeling, the feeling of sensation, the feeling of life. The Italian looking man Mr. Black Suit rushed up to me, helping me up, "We're very sorry Mr. Coufian." he said handing me my wallet which he took earlier, "We'll make this up to you."

Now Joseph you may say what kind of city is this, where something so horrible can happen to you. And let me tell you there are probably a lot of people that agree with you. But as for me, I cannot leave here, my dreams are here. I am bound by my connection to these people, the place and how it seems, especially Mr. Carletti who took so much pity on me, he gave me a job driving for him. Now whenever I go to insomnia, they completely I don't know the me, I'm treated as important, I get free drinks and I love my new do. So please Joseph I want you to see I'm doing fine and don't think I'm crazy anymore for moving here. I miss all of you. Write back soon.

Love,

Jack

P.S. Give Taline a big kiss from me!

Kent

Kent had just been to the store. He had bought a fifth of whiskey, and he had the hotel room for the night. He doesn't know how it happened, but the other night at the nudie bar, or strip club or whatever you want to call it - whatever - he had met a girl.

She was tall, too tall, maybe six foot, blonde, with short hair, not particularly cute, but she had something, something cute he doesn't know, maybe he was gay, something motherly and in a way wholesome, something benevolent, she was the bartender and not a dancer.

Once, maybe twice before he'd been at the club. To him it was just a bar, someplace to cool down and have a drink. Something to do in his long nights in his lonely suburban town. He didn't mind the girls mind you, they were just fine, maybe he knew, but what he found in that place, was more than just gawking at women. He saw in that club, something clean and tasteful going on. He thought it would have made him more uncomfortable, but it didn't.

When Kent met the bartender he only glanced at her and then she looked back with a bright, almost forced smile, a waitress like, desperate, but beautiful smile. Kent only then looked at her, noticed the lines on her face and on her forehead, the sadness and love in her eyes. He was immediately whisked off to thoughts of an ocean front hotel room in Milan, he didn't even know if they existed, but he was there with that tall beauty. He must of been smiling awkwardly at her because instead of turning away, she began to walk right towards him. Kent froze, he had seen the women talk to customers, but he never thought they would talk to him. "Do you need another beer honey?" she asked. Stupidly he responded, " Uh huh." "Another Bud?" she asked. "Yeah." was Kent's answer. There was really something about her and Kent left her what was for him a big tip.

The very next day he went in again looking for her. It was early afternoon so nobody was there and he walked strait up to the bar. A man came out from behind the room behind the bar, Kent felt: relieved, disappointed, exasperated, stupid, pleasant, forced. " You got ID?" the man asked. Kent quickly pulled out his wallet. "What you have'n?" the man then asked. "A Budweiser please." The man then opened a bottle and handed him the beer. Kent happily turned around, faced the empty stage, and leaned against the bar, drinking his beer. A few minutes later, he felt a hand on his shoulder, he turned around, "Your back again. Your the Bud guy from yesterday?" She spoke with a southern drawl, that Kent thought he could eat up like a cool glass of lemonade or a warm bowl of ice cream. "Don't mess this up, don't ruin this,... -What?" he thought and he smiled and then took a swig of his beer. A long time passed as she readied the bar, taking out towels, moving beers and replacing cups, finally he broke the silence, "Uh, what's your name?" "It's Jackie honey" she answered. "Jackie, that's nice." Kent stammered back. "Yes, it is." she said and went back to work. Eventually they got to talking. A bum came in and started to hit on her. He became their inside joke for the next few hours. "No just really me." he joked.

Later as their conversation got more intense she always gave him a soothing, "I know the feeling honey." "Thanks Jackie." was always his reply. Kent liked the way she called him honey, for a while he even entertained the idea of addressing her as baby, but as the customers began filing in he noticed a feeling of resentment arise in the customers. The normal kind of jealousy he was used to of, Why does she talk to *him?* Kent realized she got paid to talk to the customers, so he just thought, tough sh-t, to everyone else, and anyway they really had something going. But it wasn't long after when he let his emotions get the best of him and he realized the conversation couldn't go on anymore in that context. Finally he brought himself to say it.

"Jackie?"

"What is it honey, do you want another beer?"

"No, I want to ask you something."

"What is it honey?"

Kent lowered his voice and spoke softly so only she would hear, "Jackie, I want to spend the night with you. You know the whole night."

"Kent, honey, we just don't do that here."

"I really mean it."

"I know, I'm flattered, we just don't, I could lose my job." she said as she touched him on the nose. Kent began to blush.

"Jackie I know that's probably your standard answer, but we just got to, I got five hundred bucks, I know its not much, but I just want a night so we can talk." Kent didn't know why he said it or even how she would take it, but he did it, he said it. Just then a dirty man in a biker jacket called out to her, "Excuse me!" She rushed over and helped him. Kent was flush and he quietly drank his beer. He was feeling guilty and stupid all over. He was downing his beer so he could just get out of there, then Jackie came back. She handed him a piece of paper, on it, he would find out, was her phone number and the numbers eight o'clock written on it, "I'll meet you here, in back, at eight o'clock, that's when I get off. Be discrete and if you can't make it call. And for heavens sake don't be a crazy, Okay?" her words melted around his heart like butter. Kent stunned nodded finished his drink and left. The time was seven-thirty now, and Kent poured himself a drink. He had waited.

The Destination

They say the moon losing its shine because of gases released into the atmosphere. The clouds of freon 14 are heavy enough to stay on the surface and it essentially absorbs all or most of the reflectable light. A totally unbelievable explanation I think, the 40 in industry has been strip mining the moon for the past 15 years. The moons shine went in blotches, like the man in the moon's face got some disease. A cancer that slowly took over his face. It wasn't an atmospheric dim and in my opinion the 40 in industry are once again telling us lies. Stealing the moon's shine. But who knows? They don't know.

The whole issue didn't bother me much anyway, it was just, on that afternoon when I dropped off my Mom at the airport and I decided to go to the Apollo restaurant, overlooking the transport field, watching them move mountains of that grayish dust- used in everything from the filtration of our water, to the additive that lightens, strengthens and lowers the cost of all metals, paper, and now plastics.

"They should eat that." I thought as I sat there watching the whole process. It was dirty, dusty, and disgusting, guilty business, but then what job the 40 in industry does isn't, in my opinion, and the truth is anyway that we probably do eat it, along with it's other million uses. I sat there drinking one vodka after another the whole thing seemed impishly silly and substandard, it wouldn't please the you.

I went out on to the patio and ordered another. I was watching them ready a transporter that was bound for outer space. They were unloading, refueling and generally doing busy business things. I had to go to the bathroom.

As I was in there, I noticed a cupboard near the door that was slightly open. Being an idyllically curious boy I looked inside the closet. In it were some supplies: Comet, a plunger, a mop and a mop bucket, but inside the bucket, were some jumpers. The gray and red jumpers that the transport dock workers wear, and it hit me, I can go up there, do it, and see for myself. See why the moon losing its shine, and in a way, to finally know that me and the 40 are liars.

I put on the jump suit. It was a perfect fit. I laughed to myself to cover the fact that the whole thing was ludicrous, and suddenly I was having second thoughts. Then someone rapped on the door, "Is someone in there?" a woman's voice asked. "Yes ma'am, just a minute." I answered. I washed my hands and patted my face. I dried with some paper towels made with moon dust, made hyperhygenically, a new you fad, and had a long look in the mirror. I thought just breath, and opened the door with my head down and walked out. She made no notice of me and walked right into the bathroom. I still had my clothes under my arm so I asked the hostess for a bag. She promptly got one, no questions. As I left the Apollo; I left some money on the table and then looked around, no one was on the patio. I quickly hopped the fence right onto the space gateway 40 in industry tarmac.

Everywhere people were busy with the mountains of moon dust in all its different ways. No one noticed me, which was good and a bad thing I guess with terrorism and the revolution we squash. I walked over to pad five where transport workers were readying a delivery ship with supplies to aid to the moon. I grabbed a box near a conveyor and began loading. Large fork lifts were doing most of the work loading huge bundles and boxes on to the ship, I was doing small stuff. Eventually, I made my way onto the ship cleaning, things like the bathroom and checking stability on the control panel, dusting straps and reading merchandise. Another worker handed me a 40 "bonner" broom and told me to sweep out the deck. We began talking, and since I was drunk the conversation went relatively smoothly. He began to tell me how the "gray gold" almost shorted out the command system the other day, and also how he was glad they finally sent him some extra help.

"Well you never know." I said.

"You telling me, boy?" he said, "Tain't nothing in space but the sum of what you know and the beating of your heart; one failure and you could go worse than a Texas steer in a 40 in industry slaughterhouse."

"How many times you been?" I asked.

"Why, is this your first time?" he asked.

"Uh, yeah, so?" I said.

"What you do before this?"

I had to think quickly but said, "I worked for a shipping company for six years. I applied to Space Corp. because it seemed more exiting."

"Down at the docks?"

"No, a warehouse in Downtown."

"You know boy, I worked as a trucker for six years, in my old days, from the docks to Houston."

"Through Mohave." I asked trying to keep conversation going.

"Oh no. New Mexico, Arizona, El Paso, I know it all."

"How long you been flying transports?" I asked.

"Well I started my apprenticeship when I was not much older than you, son."

We kept on for more than an hour. The situation was surreal, but still I felt comfortable, like it really was my job and the work was really mine. And even though my buzz wore off and I had a headache, I felt as though I had nothing to worry about this trip. Rodger, the transport pilot, was really a good guy, born in Texas, sort of looked like Mark Twain, with a big white mustache, graying hair and a slightly stocky body. "Suit up John." Rodger said, and we got ready to make for take off. By that time, I knew the ship pretty well and my position as a moon dust transporters apprentice made me pretty confident the hair brained scheme was going to go off. I was worried about my mother though. I wondered if I was ever going to see her again and if she got to go all right. But I never lost sight of my goals, finding out why, and helping Rodger ready the ship was my ticket to the moon. He was smart and skilled worker and was good at giving orders so the whole thing went well.

The hairs on the back of my neck were beginning to stand on end, as launch time neared. I couldn't fathom how this drunken scheme had come so far. It didn't seem possible, but I was too far in it to turn back and be me. Rodger kept on going on about if it weren't for the 40 in industry none of this could be possible. He was saying how when Space Corp. got the Okay from the then alternate 40, the pooled funding made such an ambitious project, that the morally bankrupt, bull crap, do evil politicians would never had done the do, possible the you. He said before the 25 finally took over 38 years before, when they foreclosed on the government , the country was only a shadow of what it used to be, all stood; there was no apprentice system, and evil was rampant. Like in Mexico, you would have to buy officials to get anything done, you were ticketed if you walked down the street in wrong way, and people were beginning to not know. All workers were just taking licenses, Rodger didn't want to tell me about all the licenses, he said basically if you weren't already rich you had no chance of making it at all. It all changed when the 40 got the rotating presidency, no more bull or the crap politicians, just government strait from real people the corps. and the unions. Now people like us, Rodger told me, got a chance, and all we had to do was apply for guaranteed placement and a true to real life.

As we sat down and buckled ourselves in, Rodger started showing me the procedures for the pre-flight checks, and panic set in my soul. I worried, What was I doing? Was I really going to take Space Corp., #40 in industry down? They were untouchable everyone knew that, and poor Rodger doing what he was put on this Earth to do, who was I to even question? I felt I had to do, all work seemed to have intrinsic value, I didn't know how I was to be regarded. I didn't know if the whole shebang it was worth it.

We were locked and ready to go, I had no choice, I would soon know the truth about the moon if its shine was the one that really disappeared or if it was just heavy chemicals. We were on runway #5 and were to take off turn out over the Pacific and then gravi-jet into orbit en route to the moon. We taxied on to the runway. The roar of the engines grew deafening to where sound of a passing locomotive could compare and then Rodger looked at me with a wink, grabbed the control stick and squeezed. We were off, like a rock flung by a sling shot, we were on the our way. I must have turned pale because Rodger started laughing and said, "If you think that was something just wait till the gravi-jets start to know their way." I told him not to worry about me and he said, "That's the attitude we like around here." as he banked the craft out over the sea.

We arrived at lunar landing base two, a little over three hours later. It was a little crazy pulling out of the atmosphere, but once out, we made a smooth effortless slingshot way strait for the moon. Rodger didn't unbelt once the whole trip, he said bouncing around the cockpit of a transport like a jackrabbit being chased by a coyote, is only a recipe for trouble, but not listening to him I unbelted anyway and floated around more like a dust bunny in the light of an attic. When I tried to take a leak Rodger started laughing hysterically as I floated around upside down in circles trying to keep my penis up in the vacuum port. "You better clean that whiz up boy." he said through fits of laughter.

When we finally opened the airlock hatch to the moon settlement four, they welcomed us with open arms, they asked things like, "Rodger who's the new recruit?", "Rodger it's good to see ya, how you doing?", "Hey Rodge' what's the news from home?" Everywhere men, good men were busy at work. There were signs about safety, and signs promoting the 40 in industry, of course promoting their myriad of products and producings which were the only ones available in the settlement and the walls and the floor glowed. When we finished unloading the supplies Rodger gave me a pat on their back and said, "You did good today, now go and enjoy yourself for a few hours, get the feel of the place, you got a watch. You right?"

"Yeah." I answered.

"Well then be back here at 9:00 pacific time, you got it? And we'll be ready and loaded and back home in time to sleep through the morning."

"Good, I'll see you then." and then I started to walk away.

"You watch yourself boy." was his goodbye.

I said, "Okay."

We were fitted with weighted suits so the effects of the reduced gravity were less noticeable. It was strange getting around, but it wasn't long before I found the entrance to the mines, a great steel door, with a concentric smaller but still gigantic steel inset, like an automated bank safe door which I'd seen in the movies.

"Hey where you going?" cried a man from a booth carved out of the side of the gigantic aerated cavern.

"I'm with the transport, it's my first time, I want to take a look at the mines."

"It's a long walk that way. You sure?" he said.

"What?" I asked.

"The mining begins over seven stories down."

"Oh." I said dumbly.

"To get down there you got to take the elevator over here. Your going to have to sign this to get past this point."

What's it say?" I asked.

"Nothing, just that your aware of the dangers of moon dust and your aware you've been pre-selected to do this sort of work. Read it."

"Oh, of course." I said.

"Well I won't brief you then, seeing your not a important person or anything." he said.

"Yeah, there's no need. Hey buddy," I asked, "is there any truth to the freon atmosphere thing?"

"You better not go and talk like that around here, you hear me? There are 10,800 miners on the moon. Each one of 'em got a family, kids, you get what I'm saying? The 'you' is the way." he said.

"Yeah, I've been pre-qualified."

"Yeah right." he said angrily, "My daughter just had her first kid and if it wasn't for the medical collective #3 in industry I don't know if she would have ever got along." Old #3, it's a miracle, I thought to myself. "Now I can see your curious, so here's your breathing apparatus and your eye shields operate from there." he showed me how to use the equipment, Warming up he said, "I'll send you down to level nine just buzz me when you want to come back up."

"Okay." I said and stepped into the biggest elevator I had ever seen. It was cold and dusty in there and standing in the middle of that huge moving room made me feel more alone than I'd ever felt before. It moved slowly and finally the elevator slowed to a stop and the doors unlocked. I took a moment, the wide doors slid open revealing the biggest mining operation I could have ever imagined. The walls of the cave shone brilliantly, it was beautiful, there was no need for any kind of lights whatsoever. A great and multi toothed grinder was spinning and grinding the glowing moon rock into the lifeless gray dust everyone on Earth is used to, it took a minute. The dust was then spit on to a conveyer which dumped the dust into a never ending chain of railway cars. Each empty box was being filled within only a few ways.

As I walked closer to the operation I saw an army of men and bulldozers working in a beautiful but terrible harmony, some were clearing the way and making a path for the great machine to do its terrible work and still others were shoring up the walls of the cavern making it safe to continue. I stood in awe, mesmerized by the melding of men and machine. The loud drone of all the tools in use rang in my head. As I walked further out on to the work site I saw some men on a break, when they looked at me, I walked over. My stunned appearance became a topic of joking and conversation.

"First time huh?" one of the men jibed. All the men laughed. "We got a virgin over here, I'm going show you my drill." another man screamed, pointing to me, to the railroad engineer. Everyone laughed once again. After some conversation I learned about the men. It seemed everyone was married, but had an ex. Uniformly they all hated their ex-wives. They all loved their kids, but the digging, being part of the great ballet of mining is what made their lives, its what made them happy. "During your three months up here, there is no world, only you, the guys and this life. It's what makes us special, we live." one of the men I talked to revealed. Some were serious, some were funny, but all had work, and that was good. I looked at my watch and it was already past eight, so I said a heartfelt goodbye to whoever I was talking and the glowing fading walls,; and was on my way up the elevator. I thought of John and Tom and Sam all guys I'd met while on break. I was down there for almost two hours. Like the rest of them I had become accustomed to the glow of the rock and the hum of the machines. It loses some kind of vigor, I guess, I wonder if the shine will regenerate, the story is, completely, looks like a lie. I figure when they crush with it it loses some molecular purity and turns slowly a dead gray, I'm sure someone at the 40 in industry has figured it really out.

On the way back me and Rodger laughed about stories I told and the stories I'd heard down in the mines. When we got off work, I quietly slipped away. I slept that morning clear into the afternoon and that very day I applied for a job at the industry, Space Corp.in particular, #39 in industry. Immediately they put me in a white room and I interviewed. I took 'em for a ride. I had to take the test. They called me in two days and told me I was just the right age to start a life as a industry man and told me to come in to pick from my positions.

So now I have a job. I dropped out of school, have a trade and found my true calling. I'm a bit not right, right? Right now I work at transporter control, I am not yet cleared for the mines on the moon, but soon I will. The funny thing is when I tell my story of the moon and its shine, people just laugh at me, and I don't blame them. They think I was hallucinating or telling them my dream or was just dreaming, but I know the truth and in time, I guess, I'll learn to keep it to myself, the shine is losing itself. Those of you that are still anti-40 in industry may think I'm crazy, I don't do you, some of you may even believe me about the moon and all, but the truth is, things change, everything changes its, and whether it's the seasons, the moon rock or even how we appreciate life, it all is, in a sense, The will. The will of god maybe, but the will of the way it should be. Although I think someday they'll repair it. Its somewhere in the bible I guess, I don't know.

THE DNA MURDERS

At a recent family gathering my cousin J.P., who is a peace officer, began to tell a story from work in a round of joke telling. We were laughing about the someone of some poor slob who never wanted to get married, but almost ended up marrying an ass, which why we laugh, all men who get married are. That's when I noticed J.P. wasn't laughing, aside I asked him what's wrong, thinking it was stuck marriage or kids trouble or something, but then he got somber and he went into his story:

"Chuck I'll tell you. The chief told us to keep a wrap on this so I've told nobody, not even Ellen." Ellen was his wife of ten years. J.P. was a stocky man, but tall, a little over weight. He had few friends outside the force. His years as an MP in the service had given him an upright, respectful, but forceful tone and he had been an LA police officer for six years. I knew he wanted to move up and become a detective. Personally, I had never seen him like this before, I took a sip from my scotch and I said, "Go on." and he continued, "It all began about six months ago, in Santa Monica, on Fourth and Arizona. A Pure-Beauty hair salon was broken into. It was a purely amateur job, hastily committed and poorly executed, or at least that's what I thought. The burglar broke the

front glass with a brick from a planter just outside the establishment, he dashed in, and

frantically searched for the safe. When I got there the place was a little messy, we got the

call from the alarm company around three in the morning. I proceeded to call the owner,

a woman who lived in an apartment in Beverly Hills, and waited for her to arrive. It was

all pretty standard. When she got there I explained we would do everything possible to

catch the burglar, but the truth was, it seemed nothing really was taken, the thief didn't

get out the safe, and the odds of catching and prosecuting the guy was minimal. She said

because of all the transient traffic in the area it had happened before and she had cameras

installed. I told her I'd be back in the morning to take the report. I didn't review the

video or even take it in for evidence.

In the morning at the end of my shift I stopped by the salon, I took the report, just

a few hundred dollars of equipment was taken and the place was torn apart in an search

for the safe. When I asked to see the video her face changed, she said I left it recording

through the night and it automatically rewound and taped over the affair, she didn't know

it did that until this morning. I explained the odds of catching the burglar to her; and I

told her it wasn't a big deal. When I asked her if she reviewed the tape the night before,

she said she did and gave me a description of a tall thin man wearing as beanie low on his

face. She told me she couldn't tell, because of the lighting, the race of the perp. Once

again I explained it wasn't a big deal and we would do everything possible to catch the

burglar. When I got back to the station I was tried, but I still filled out the report,

thinking it would just be filed away and that was that, but the shit hit the me much less

the fan.

That same morning at around five a man broke into a house off Corbin here in the Valley. The victim was brutally torn from her bed and beaten to death right in her living room."

"I heard about that." I said.

"Yes, but what you didn't hear was that the whole house was littered with foreign DNA material, hair clippings and nail shavings…, items that can be found in a hair salon. The whole department was a mess, we didn't publicize the details of the murder from fear of copycat murders and the investigation was a wash because the whole crime scene was tainted, this guy was smart. And of course with the whole department looking for a scapegoat where do they look, right at me and the salon break in. I meant the question was there, where did the assailant get the genetic material, that was the key, did he know, and time and time again my salon break in came up. They are going over my investigation with a fine tooth comb and it didn't take much to see I did a shoddy job on whole. I lost the video, I wrote a vague report, I didn't call in for finger prints, I didn't try, I wrote a shotty report of how but not my of to find witnesses, according to the detectives on the murder case I didn't do anything correctly. I tell you, my job, my future, my life, it's all under review right now, is it I." around now some of my family began to get involved and listen, they do, "I don't know if I don't know, am I Hopi? Will I'll still be doing this in the next few months."

"J.P. I'm sorry." I said, while getting mad at the rest, "But, for sure that can't be the only place the murderer could have gotten his material."

"It's hard to tell, DNA tests are expensive and hundreds if not thousands are going on right now, we do do I not know, after this mess I felt the only is, is to do everything thoughroly." he said as he put on his shocks glasses, "We're trying to see if we can get an address out of one of them, have a way. Only felons have registered DNA and some public workers. As it stands right now the detectives have got a big fat zero and in a bad way that's still good for me. Please Chuck don't tell anyone, I'm hoping it'll just take care of itself."

"No, don't worry about me, I do." I said and then continued, "You guys have an APB out on the guy in the video?"

"We want him for questioning, but what we got later from the owner of the salon was minimal. I look like a doe." J.P. said.

"So what else are you guys doing, does the victim have a husband, or family or a boyfriend?" I went, I know.

"She had a husband who lived with her, but he was away on business in Texas, That night he was staying over a family member's house. They just moved out here a year ago."

"Is that it, all contingencies are taken care, How is he taking it?" I went.

"Terribly." was his answer.

"So the killer staked out her house or knew her and knew she'd be alone. Did she have many friends or was a regular somewhere?" I went.

"No. She was a loner. She didn't work. Just talked in rare. You got to see her house aside from all the blood, it was beautiful, arching trellises, plants and even a full blown vegetable garden. Her husband says the weather and the soil is the only thing that made her happy here in Los Angeles." J.P. went.

"This is a tough case." I said quietly to J.P., "What about the hair material?"

"Don't go there." J.P. did, "I've been around town after work. I've been to barber shops, salons, everywhere I could think of, nobody has been giving away hair clippings and they all have locked trash cans. Nobody in this day and age wants a problem; I did. And just to think of covering up the crime in this way you'd need access, you'd need to know someone, to know."

"And of course someone who knew the victim too." I did.

"Maybe, there's a lot of maybes. The detectives have checked out as many salons as they can so far, employees, owners. They started in the valley and now their moving on, its been six months. Basically everyone with a record, in this case, or even big enough to commit the crime has been checked out, so far nothing. And the murderer was really cruel, the savageness of the beating was unlike anything we'd seen. Like he pummeled her with his bare hands hours after she was dead. We do. Let me tell you there wasn't much left, this guy was a sadistic misogynist." I could see the disgust and anger in J.P. eyes as he finished up what he said, he loved his job, wanted to be a detective and I wanted to help him, but I was at a loss. Then my sister announced coffee and pastries in the dinning. We got up and went to go eat, but neither of us had an appetite for dessert or do, we sat. That night, when we said our goodbyes I told J.P. to call me whenever he wanted and I was ready to help, he said thanks and that was that.

I mulled the story around in my head for the next few days. I was sure it was a lover or a boyfriend and not that mystery stranger in the lost video. And that Tuesday the killer struck again. On the news I heard that another women had been murdered in Canoga Park Hill. She was beaten, dragged and I knew I was being lied to when it was said an unrelated death. Given the proximity to the other killing I was sure it was the same man. When I heard, my horror, on Wednesday I called J.P. he said, "Hi,"

"J.P. how are you?" I said.

"You heard." J.P. said.

"Was it, I mean was it the DNA murder?" I asked.

"Same M.O. DNA material all over the crime scene it s a secret. The woman alone, and beaten and dragged her to a pulp." J.P. said.

"How terrible, it seems the killer has got a taste for blood. At least your off your hook by now." I said.

"Why?" he asked.

"It's simple he's got to be from the valley, in old hill, three tree and he never could have stolen that much hair and such in that one robbery in Santa Monica, this man has a source." I confidently said.

"Interesting, I know." he answered.

"Know. It's more than a possibility that you've got a serial killer on your hands. Anyway, I've got to go, but you look free to me, I have a computer class tonight. I'll call you tomorrow." I said.

"Okay see you, my doe." he said.

"Keep me informed. Bye." and I hung up. I was late for my computer class at my local west valley occupational school.

On the way I began thinking to myself maybe the department had got it all wrong. The occupational center had a beauty teaching college, and it was in the vicinity of the crimes. I thought I'd better check it out.

When I arrived at the occupational center my class was already started, but as how to finesse a windows app, to me, wasn't half as interesting as J.P.'s dilemma, I *know,* I went strait to the beauty school. When I climbed up the bungalow stairs, my own drama, I entered into a skinny hallway flanked by offices on the right and lime green linoleum tile on the floor, which to me seemed okay, but to my family a senses insult that would seem okay. On the left at the end of the hallway was a large room, with rows of salon chairs, driers and manicure tables. The room was buzzing with activity: a teacher, a beautiful thin woman with shaded blonde and red streaks in her hair, was walking around helping out the students in giving styling and haircuts to a myriad of clients, friends, I guess, of the students. The walls were lined with mannequin heads and like any beauty school hairs with varying hair styles. The front wall had a mirror with shaved, styled and unshaven mannequins' heads. After a time, the teacher noticed me and walked over, she said, "Can I help you?"

"Yes,, in a bit, but I can see your busy" I retorted, "are you giving haircuts today?"

"Yes, but did you come from twentieth century English Lit,?" the thin woman joked back, "or did you find your way here by reading our ad? For two weeks a semester we give away free haircuts."

"You've been cutting hair here since Monday?" I asked a bit nervous.

"We cut hair here the seventeenth and eighteenth weeks of each semester. Were all booked up for today but if you come back tomorrow we can take you then." she said in belief.

"Thank you ma'am. Where should I sign up?" I said finding my way.

"You can do it over the phone or go right there to the second office on the left." she said. It was a place with little privacy, with wire covered windows and an office you can barely make out.

I went into the office and found that the beginners and the advance students alike cut hair in the seventeenth and eighteenth weeks which was now, the styling ended that Friday. I made an appointment for Friday before my class, I wanted to ask if they given any nail shaving away, would they believe me? I had no idea that the end of the semester was so near. I then went into the main office and asked for a schedule of classes for the last two semesters, they thought it was odd, so I made up a story that I needed the dates and codes of my class for a job interview, they believe. They quickly dug up the schedules out of some file. And then I went to my computer class, my wonderful, inequitable, computer class.

When I got home that night I was sure I had solved the case. When I calculated the weeks from the previous two semesters, spring fell from about June fifth to about the twentieth, and fall was six months before during the holidays around December fifth to the twentieth. I knew in the bones of my heart the first murder would fall inside these dates and the killer was, with this definite proof of date, in reach, but would they believe me? They murder when the DNA is active.

The next day I called J.P. and left a message, he was at work and out in the field. I was anxious, but realized he didn't have loads of free time to waste on me and he didn't know what I know. The problem was I was close, and they wouldn't believe this I, I couldn't concentrate on anything else.

I called him again that evening. The DNA murder… His mother answered the phone, she was at his house babysitting the kids while he and Ellen went out to a movie and din. I of course got into a twenty minute conversation with her which ended with, tell J.P. to call me as soon as possible. The next day I was getting my haircut in the class and I wanted J.P. to be there. I didn't know what I was looking for, but I was sure I would.

I went to the trade school right after work, at the hardware store, and the day classes were in their final leg. I went to go sign in for my haircut. As I made a right to the office where I signed up, I noticed a big figure, the DNA murderer?, standing behind me. I turned round to see, and there he was a gigantic man big in all forms, stature, size and height true American. He was dressed in a cusdodian blue jump suit. His large fingers were wrapped around a broom handle making it look like a dolly toy, pipe of half inch. He had a loose mop of straight light brown hair about his head and his head to be sure was quite large, as big as the mop of his head, and looked small, round, and out of place upon that large frame of his.

When he looked at me from his work I was struck to the bone, I didn't know. I looked down at me and went into their place for work.

"I'm here for a haircut." I told the administrator.

"Name please." the woman said.

"Chuck." I said and she took out the ledger and crossed out my name.

"A student will be with you in just a moment." she said. It went smoothly, I guess, *they* got to do something about me.

"Excuse me," I said, "who is that man sweeping up the hair in there?"

"He is an imposing man isn't he?" she said as she looked at me.

"Over there, I couldn't help but notice." I said, and now she is going to tell me he is as gentle as a lamb.

"Well he is as gentile as a lamb. His name is Michael. He is a janitor here at the beauty school. He's been with us for more than two years and we just love him here. We call him Big Mike."

"Gentile as a lamb? Is he I?" I said as she was ushering me out of the office. We must of got the attention of the teacher because as we entered the hallway she came right over and grabbed me by the arm.

"I'm happy to see you've come back." pale blonde, red highlights, she was she easy to look at. She was the same teacher from the other night. She sat me down in one of those chairs. Only a few of the students were available. There were kids cutting hair, blow drying, doing manicures and even a back room for what I assume was waxing. It was like a real salon only more dingy, more linoleum and more crowded. Big Mike was the most likely suspect but I couldn't be sure so I kept a keen eye out upon the students. Most in the class were women; to me they were out, they couldn't produce the savageness of heart and the brute force needed for the killings. If I snooped would they believe me?

The men in the class were small, to say the least. Most were gay to me, light foots I thought. I had my eyes on the room/office wondering why, when I met my stylist. What I first noticed was that she was a he! He had a skinny bony face and a skinny bony body, he was tall and had a big bush of dark curly regular hair on his head. His mannequin was shaved clean, and scary, did he know?

"I hope you know how to use those." I nervously didn't joke.

He didn't take kindly to the comment, "They tell me I do, but I don't believe them." he said.

Say what? I thought, "Well, in that case just be careful." I said, " I like it short. On the sides a number, I don't know and medium long on top and don't forget to clean the back."

"Go ahead." he said.

I looked the boy up and down as he was cutting my hair. He seemed the type; quiet with hidden monsters inside, and I noticed his hands, they were red and bruised with sores on the knuckles. I had to find out more about him.

"You must have been in quite a fight. I couldn't help but notice your hands." I said.

"It's nothing, the gym I belong to has a kickboxing class, I guess I went to hard on the bag." he said. The DNA murderer?

" I see. Why's a kid like you in beauty school?" I said.

"A job." he said flatly and then clamed up, like I pissed him off or something. Quite a while went by before we exchanged words again. He had me turned away from the mirror into the class which seemed innocent.

"You ever had your hair cut and styled before?" he broke the silence while taking out the blow-drier.

"No." I answered, "I have never even had my hair blow-dried before." and then that's when I peeked into the mirror; my hair was butchered. It had short bangs and hung all different lengths about my head like a broom. I wads horrified for sure, but I was sure this boy was exhibiting his latent tendencies to take out in surge out in anger, only he took it out on my hair. I said, "Don't you think son it should be even?"

"This is the latest." he replied, "With some gel I'm going to recommend to you and a blow dry your friends won't even recognize you."

I didn't know, "Do you think, not even my mother, that, my friend, is what I'm afraid of." I said. And then he proceeded to fashion my hair into a spiky mohawky mélange, quite stylish, but totally unappropriate. When I finally saw the finished creation I couldn't help but hold back a laugh, so much so in fact, that my eyes teared up and the boy reacted like a wounded seven year old.

"I'm sorry sir, if you don't like it that much Mrs. Laller can fix it." he said half angry, half upset.

"No, don't worry about it. What's your name?" I had asked him before, but he didn't answer.

"Bobby Thomson." he said.

"Good, Bobby, I think you've taken ten years away from me. Now I'm in my youth, I thank you" I said and then continued, "By the way what do you think of that janitor? Is he a violent guy?"

"I don't know." Bobby said.

"All right, thank you very much." I said and left. I was trying not to notice all the cock-eyed looks I was getting from the other students. As soon as I was outside I called my barber, "Not until Monday, I'm going out right now." he said and I made an appointment for Monday, I took it easy. Mad and suspicious of that boy I drove around to the back of the beauty school and waited.

It only took fifteen minutes for the class to let out. I spotted Bobby leaving the class, my plan was to follow him to see if I could get any clues.

He drove a gray Chevy Cavalier an older model but in good condition. I followed him out of the parking lot, my computer class was going to suffer slow and incapable. He left the school and got on the freeway. We got on the 134 and got off in Burbank. His home was far out of the way of the old hill, but you never really can trust somebody from Burbank, so I kept on him, I sat and waited. After about twenty minutes, and after I had completely cleaned all the dust off my dashboard with a rag, my phone rang.

"Yes?" I answered.

"It's J.P."

"J.P. I got some news for you," I said exited, "the case is almost solved. Not only are you saved, but your gonna get a promotion."

"Wait, slow down, what are you taking about?" he stammered out.

"It started on Wednesday at the occupational center after our phone call..." I said and I explained to him about the haircuts and the seventeen and eighteen weeks.

"And?" J.P. didn't get it.

"And when exactly was the first murder?" I asked.

"I'll never forget that night, it was Friday December the tenth." J.P. said.

"Precisely, just as I thought. The seventeenth week of that semester began on the fifth." I said. "they correlate."

"Oh my G-d." J.P. muttered.

"Yes, both murders correlate with the West Valley Occupational Center's schedule. It's unbelievable. And now I'm on his tail, at one of the suspects houses."

"Are you crazy? You don't know what you could be getting yourself into." J.P. said.

"Don't worry J.P. his name is Bobby Thomson and I tell you this boy is shady, he even had bruises on his hands. I followed him here, he doesn't even know" I said.

"Where are you, do you know your not allowed to. I'm coming right over." J.P. said and I gave him directions. I also told him there was another suspect an employee, but he told me to sit on it, and we'd talk later.

He arrived not half an hour later. There was no movement outside of the house up to that point. Inside things were going on, but through the curtains I couldn't make out much. When J.P. got there something was ready to happen. I flashed my headlights to show J.P. where I was parked, cat and dagger, he parked his car and got into mine. As soon as he got into my car it started.

"What's with the hair?, Do you know?" he said holding back laughter and doing a bad job of it.

He was mad I retorted back but it was a no try, "It's a long story, but it's that bastard in there that did it." I said.

"So what exactly have you got?" He asked and I told him the complete story of the class and about Big Mike custodian extraordinaire.

"It really could be any L.A. occupational school." he said expressing doubts.

"Yes, but this school is in the direct vicinity of the crimes." I said.

"If it's true I've got to call this in." he said. I begged him to wait and then Bobby appeared out the front door of his house, "I'm saved." But that's what I thought.

"That's him." I said.

"He's so thin." J.P. said.

"But he's tall and you never know with his type." I said thinking about the guys latent anger and self loathing that he must have for attempting to become a hairdresser. He was dressed in sweats and had a gym bag. We followed him to a L.A. Fitness. We watched for a half hour as he spent his time in the window on a treadmill, then he went back into the gym. J.P. decided to pose as an interested gym patron and went inside to take a better look at him. With the free time I had I thought I'd check out his car.

He left his doors unlocked and when I went to open the door the door went "crrack". My heart racing I looked around as if the gym goers in the parking lot were going to be suspicious of a man opening an open car door. When I looked inside I found nothing out of the ordinary. Generally the car was neat and clean. In his glove box he had thrown in some trash and there was his registration, but nothing else not even a screwdriver. When I lowered his back seats to get in his trunk there was nothing, no plastic bags, no blood, no mess, no hair. I was beginning to think I was chasing the wrong guy. When J.P. got back to my car he confirmed my suspicions.

"He's not our guy." J.P. said.

"Why?" I asked.

"He doesn't fit the M.O. He was friendly with all the girls and they were friendly with him. The DNA murder. Plus there was a kick boxing class and when the teacher came out to ask him why he wasn't participating, I heard him say he went at it to hard the last time, which confirms his story." J.P. seemed sure he upped me. I was sure too.

"I went through his car, there was nothing there. No signs of him going through anything especially traumatic, no mess, no blood, there was nothing at all, I think your the right." I said.

"I didn't tell you to go through his car." J.P. said, " I hope you know that was highly illegal and unethical to me."

"Lets don't worry now, we have a killer to catch. I say lets go back to the school and check out this Mike guy." I proposed out and J.P. bit lip.

"Lets go, but lets take it easy, I just want to take a look around before I call this information in." J.P. said.

"This is crazy, you know that." I joked.

"Don't test me before I change my mind. Just take me back to my car and lets go." J.P. said.

I said Okay and I we drove back to the school.

We got to the occupational center a little after eight. Classes weren't over until nine thirty which meant Big Mike was there until at least ten P.M. When we met in the parking lot J.P. told me to follow his lead. We went to the main office and J.P. had a flash of brilliance.

"Excuse me." J.P. said, "I'm with John Peterman and son were here about the remodel of the beauty school.

"Yes." the woman in the office said.

"Yes, were biding the remodel and we were informed that the janitor could show us around." J.P. said.

"You know, no one tells us anything around here and the principle is not in..." The woman went on. J.P. interrupted.

"I know, they rarely tell the people in the office anything, we just need a moment so we can take some measurements." and J.P. produced a tape measure.

"Well I'll call the janitor Mike Boykowski to come and help you." the woman said. J.P. quickly produced a pad of paper and wrote down the name. The woman rang the school bell twice. "What's your name sir?" the woman asked.

"John." J.P. answered.

"Okay John, you two can have a seat right over there. Mr. Boykowski will be with you shortly." the woman said and we sat down.

"Brilliant." I said to J.P.

"Just be cool, son." J.P. said to me, "Your lucky with that hair I even brought you along."

"That's enough pop, I know at your age things can be pretty stressful." I said as Big Mike was coming in. He went over to the office desk and started a conversation with the attendant. We got up. It bothered people, why you two. Do they have a right? You could hear Mike say things like why didn't they tell me about this? And then just cave in, Okay, he said.

"Do you men have a card?" woman asked.

"Of course," I said thinking fast, "there in the truck. Past the make up test sign. I'll bring one in as soon as we're finished. It will only be a minute, we don't want to trouble you."

"And you are?" she asked.

"The son." I said keeping a strait face.

"Okay, just make sure and get that card to me." the woman said.

"We find a way." J.P. said just trying to shut me up.

When we left the office J.P. started asking questions.

"The beauty school is in the building?:" J.P. asked.

"In bungalows four, five, and six." Big Mike the custodian answered.

"Is it always pretty busy in there?" J.P. went on.

"Yeah, it's busy in there, especially now, we take a three week break in two weeks then summer school starts." Big Mike said.

"It's been Busy, why?" J.P. asked.

"It's the end of the year they always cut hair in there this time of year." Mike said.

"It must be a lot of work. It must get in your nerves and all." J.P. asserted.

"Me, naw." Big Mike said.

"I bet cleaning up all that hair must get annoying." J.P. said trying to get a sense of the big man and he got to him.

"You know what's annoying? Dambed teachers asking favors all the time. The work don't bother me its all that other crap." Mike answered.

"What would we do without us a days work." I said, Big Mike turned and looked at me. He had a stern, but gentile face. J.P. continued.

"So anyway, what kind of favors the teachers asking you to do?" he said.

"You know, the usual clean up this, move that. The other day I had eight bathrooms to finish and the drafting professor had me move a whole closet full of computers to a room down the hall, just to move them back for the computer science professor the next night. Its things like that that tick me off. There just isn't enough time in the day - I say." Mike said.

"You have a temper do you?" J.P. said.

"Me? Naw." Mike said.

When we arrived at the beauty school we realized that Big Mike was doing his final clean up of the place. As we walked around we noticed Big Mike was putting the cut hair and floor mess into a separate trash bag. Suddenly my senses came to me and fear settled in the pit of my stomach. I quietly turned to J.P. pointing and stammered out, "He's our man." J.P. put his hand over mine and lowered my hand. He walked over to Big Mike and I noticed a gun butt in the small of his back behind his shirt. "We're done here." he said and looked at me, I was concentrating on the walls. He then continued inching his hand toward the small of his back, "You always do that, put the organic stuff in a separate bag?"

"Naw," Mike said, "for the last few years the computer animation teacher asks me to save this for some project of his. Every year he goes on about his gallery project - I tell you there just ain't enough time in the day."

J.P. looked at me again and I looked at him, "That's it." he said and continued, "You know I got a hunch that that computer teacher won't be bothering you much in the future."

"What do you mean?" Mike said giving a supremely strange look at J.P.

"Nothing, I just heard that computer animation has no future." J.P. said.

"Oh." Mike said and he showed us out to the parking lot.

The next day Mike was taken in for questioning and the computer animation professor, a Jack Johnson, was arrested on suspicion of murder. J.P. got promoted to detective and me - I ended up dropping out of my aggravating computer class, the sum is them and not me.

TWO MOUNTAINS AND A VALLEY

It was many years ago, in a far off land called Thousand Oaks. I can't remember why I was there, maybe it was to go to the Thousand Oaks Auto Mall or maybe I was there running an errand to eat at a Chevy's with a friend of mine, I don't remember, at least I don't remember that well. But the things I do remember I do cherish, there's more to it, I know, but its all beside the point. We were there and we were hungry, so we went into the most obvious eatery, on probably their most main street,; we went to a McDonalds.

Inside we(me and my friend) sat down to eat what was then their delectable specials, like a 99cent bacon cheese burger, with McDonalds special reconstituted bacon piece, the size of the bun, some of their wonderful fries, and a drink. As soon as we sat my friend noticed the Captain. He was wearing a dark blue Pea Jacket, scruffy beard, tanned, worn and weathered face, and a dark blue captains hat on his head. He was sitting in his corner, chain smoking Drum rollie cigarettes, which never left his lips except to put the old one in the ashtray and insert a new one into the permanent gap that opened in the side of his mouth, perfect for the size of a cigarette, like somehow he had learned to overcome natural selection and create a characteristic beneficial to his lifestyle within his lifetime.

Me and my friend went over to talk. He was a sailor, at a time, a captain of a ship, he told us stories so closely reminiscant to Conrad it made me wonder why not all people tell stories of their lives and lives past, of myths and farces. He was retired now and was staying with his daughter, miserably bored.

We stayed in that McDonalds for more than an hour, we were running late, in fact now I'm pretty sure it was a work errand, we were all smoking; I was smoking my Marlboros, my friend was smoking his Lucky Strikes, and the Captain was smoking his Drums, it was back in the time when you could sit in a restaurant after you were done, talk, smoke, and enjoy yourself. Finally I asked him, "How do you roll such perfect cigarettes?" He said it was easy, "first you make two mountains, like that, and a valley in between," he looked strait at me as he mounded two heaps of tobacco where his thumbs would go, and a depression toward the middle of the cigarette, "and then you just wrap it around like that." We all laughed, "that's the easy part huh?" And then he got serious and we got serious too, so we said goodbye to the old man and we were off.

Tens of thousands of cigarettes later and the countless thousands of cigarettes I've rolled, I probably wouldn't wish the habit on anyone, at least not in this climate. Hell having papers and baggies for cigarettes in your glove compartment never fail causes problems when you get pulled over, but there is something in cigarettes, something good. In every puff there is a little taste of Mars and it makes you happy and addicted and I'll probably get cancer for promoting such a habit, but that not what I mean to do. I mean to say, remember the Captain and me and the millions of other poor slobs out there who would rather have a cigarette than blow their brains out on some Thousand Oaks McDonalds table after taking out some kids, Mexican workers, some fat ladies, and that beautiful girl in the tight fitting sweats, fresh from the gym, putting on some make-up while she's waiting for a chocolate shake. Now I think I'll go have a cigarette, this is my last one... maybe.

PROSE AND POETRY FROM EXILE

On a trip to Montana in a little town in the foothills of the Rockies I came across an interesting bunch in a corner cafe' on the Main street of the mountain town.

I stopped in for some tea, hot tea, which was hot, which was my custom in the afternoon. Inside there was Grateful Dead playing over the stereo and a group of hippies sitting and talking, and I was wondering if they would wouldn't know. On the pine paneled walls were abstract paintings of various quality and when I finally sat down the Wolf that was Dire was ending and beginning into a drum solo. The whole time I could hear the young people's conversation. Really just a young lady wearing tight jeans and a small tied died shirt was doing most of the talking. She had a white belly which ever so slightly hung out over her jeans and I thought about it casually, earring in her belly button. The two boys with her weren't dressed radically but still had that tied died hippie, long hair edge in their appearance; they were both small men and were listening like gentlemen to the lady speaking. She, although she didn't know it, was speaking about what all young ladies talk about, men. She was having a problem with one of the guys in town, I assumed he was a mutual friend of all of theirs. It seemed he was refusing it and she was at a loss. She wasn't able to do anything artistic, including her beloved photography, she was hopeless (marriage was what we want). The boys were trying to tell her, he was just like that. I couldn't help myself, I broke into the conversation. I had to help her out.

"Excuse me, I'm sorry, but I couldn't help but overhear your conversation, but you see my lady your problem is this boy doesn't take you seriously and you desperately want him to, I don't know. You see this problem is bigger than you and this boy, you need to examine yourself." I said.

"Are you an artist?" she asked.

"Why?" I questioned.

"Because you don't look like a hunter or a fisherman. Why else would you be here, this is Boman home of the Stepton collective and its writings." she said.

"I'm just a traveler, working on a book." I said.

"Everybody here is trying to be the next Jack London, I myself am a writer." she said."

"And I'm sure your very good, but you see the man you keep taking about seams to me more like a conquest than a true meeting of the minds of you and I." they started to get interested but laugh, I continued, " If your not interested than I don't have to go on." I went.

"No, no go on." she said not really looking at me, but one of her friends.

"I see, well its like your taking a photograph, not only do you have to see the picture, you have to push the button, go for it, and capture it, the beauty you leave still exists even after you leave; you want him to think your the conquest, not the other way around. Anyway, Good Loving was beginning on the stereo, if I'm right you have nothing to lose." I finished but didn't know.

"Far out." one of the men seated with her said. The drum solo was continuing "Oh yeah, I love this part." the boy said and they all stopped started listening.

"Pardon," I broke in again a few moments later, "what's a group like yours, the Stepton Collective doing here in Montana?"

"Haven't you heard?" the young woman said.

"Yes a little, tell me." I said.

"It was here in Bosman, that Ambrose Hunt found Stepton, the name he had given to his cabin. You see, in 1920 Hunt disillusioned by society and the way life was changing in America, Pennsylvania and especially Pittsburgh, set out to the yet untamed country to the west. Eventually he found himself here in Bosman Montana. At that time though there wasn't much, and from scratch he taught himself how to survive. With little or no contact with the outside world he spent the next thirteen years up here in the wilderness. He thought himself in permanent exile, from people, from society, from the way of life that we would call human. Slowly though, his peace was found out and life came knocking at his cabin door; fur traders and huntsman began to use his cabin, which he called Stepton, as a place to find rest and shelter. He didn't know.

"What they found was extraordinary, not only did he survive but he survived well. He had grown comfortable and well suited to life out in the wilderness and his home slowly became a favorite stop for people in the area. Hunt, developed ways to make everything himself, including paper and ink, which he made from tree bark and a kind of raspberry. With his simple tools and his solitude he created an entire imaginary world. His writings and drawings became well known in the mountain community here in Montana.

"When scholars back east heard of the Blake of the west his fame grew even more, but he never published in fact he never let anyone even see any of his illuminated writings unless you were able to visit Stepton, which few at the time were really able to do. They say his insights on human nature and society as a whole were worth any man's time, but the few who had seen his work were all outdoorsman able to make the journey.

"Eventually a scholar hired a guide and made his way up to the cabin. He was the son of a wealthy, powerful banker who never quite understood his father. He spent a few weeks at Stepton in the spring of '36. He came back so enthusiastic about Hunt that he decided to buy all the land surrounding Stepton and start an arts community. His dad gave him the money, but under false pretences. As soon as the land was secured, the father John Bosman sent a dozen of his henchman to this place and started the town of Bosman. The town flourished, logging and fur trading took hold and Ambrose Hunt gathered up all his things and fled higher into the mountains, never to be seen again. And with the winters up there most people think he didn't survive that first winter. But his life and his spirit did go on and to this day Bosman is the arts capital of Montana." and she finished her story.

"He was quite a man." I said.

"There's more on him in the library." one of the boys said to me. The Grateful Dead finished their concert and a Doors album started playing. I was done with my tea and said my goodbyes and left.

When I got home I was refreshed from the mountain life and even though I spent most of my time there in the library for a while I felt like the heart of that community. I wondered about the girl, she knew better than me, I assume, And every night I saw her there in that cafe' conversing with a different guy, but in my heart of hearts I know she was alone, maybe as alone as Ambrose Hunt.

Leda and the Swans

Will was sitting, playing some scales on the guitar, when the buzzer rang. Randy was sitting watching TV and I, Leda was up in the bedroom on the phone. We didn't know, Will looked at Randy who was not moving, even though he was closer to the door and he knew Leda wasn't going to move from the telephone. When the buzzer rang again Will got up and answered, annoyed but silent.

"Yeah?"

"This is Oscar, I'm the bassist. I was referred to you by Angela."

"Yap, I'll buzz you in, 3B on the third floor."

"Yeah, I got it." Oscar said and Will buzzed him in and went back to his guitar. I knew, and when they heard the knocking at the door Will said, "Randy could you please get it?"

"It's open." Randy yelled not moving from the couch. Oscar opened the door and came in. It was a strictly industrial space, about a thousand sq. foot, with concrete floors. There was a lone tweed like couch beige with brown, green, and orange stripes facing a small television on top of a milk carton. In the corner was a small kitchenette and in the back there was a spiral staircase leading up to a platform second floor. It had four ten foot by ten foot tall windows which were frosted white and were tilted toward the street. There was musical instruments and various recording equipment on folding chairs and a laptop set up on a fold out table. Will was sitting on his amp holding his guitar and Randy still unmoved was on the couch, how did he know? Damn box owns that guy.

"Hello, I'm Oscar." he announced as he entered the room, I liked him very much. He was carrying a black nylon case which contained his bass. He was taller, muscular, but a little overweight. He had thin, chin length brown hair and a smallish looking round face.

"I'm Will, this is Randy, the drummer, and Leda's upstairs." Will said.

"Yeah, I know, Cool." Oscar said.

"How long you been playing bass?" Will asked, what a dweeb.

"Oh, I don't know, two years, ever since I moved to LA." Oscar replied.

"Let me play you our demo, so you can see what we're about. Leda! I know your up there," Will yelled and then went over to the lap top which spit out their music over one of the amps. Our music was punk, with driven drums and distortion and then would get soulful and funky. Will understood the blues and when he jammed you could hear it, but the highlight was Leda's voice, I was rough and demanding but mousy and somehow said, 'We don't take ourselves too seriously' Oscar wondered how they ever got picked up as a punk band without a bassist, but he saw they had crossover potential, and the money he always dreamed of was in reach. He went over to Randy and sat down. Oscar said something to Randy and then got up and went over to the mini-fridge and got out two beers, Randy called out, "Don't forget the pretzels, they're right there in the corner." Oscar grabbed the chips and started to make his way back to the couch, when he saw Leda walking down the stairs.

She was a beauty, to be seen, to be believed, and he knew immediately how this band had been picked up. She had an oval face, with emerald eyes and straggly streaked blonde hair. She was thin and had thin lips, she looked like a Viking goddess, pure and innocent, gone bad. Her white bare feet shone from out of her loose fitting casual black pants and he watched her figure descend the stairs in a loose fitting pink tee-shirt which ever so lightly clung to her breasts, I knew he noticed me.

"Hi." Oscar said.

"Hello." Leda answered and then turned to Will, "We're all set up for tonight, at the Dragonfly it's a local club, I think you can find our way."

"I've been practicing a new song." Will answered angered.

"Well give it to Oscar, let see if he can play." Leda said.

"It's no problem, I can play." Oscar said opening his beer and handing the other to Randy. He sat down on the back rest of the couch looking at Leda. He noticed me, Will didn't, he handed him the music written out like a symphony, with each musicians part spelled out and notated. I do not know.

"What's this?" Oscar asked.

"It's the new song." Will answered.

"What the fuck is this? I can't read this." Leda and Randy began laughing, "You guys are shitting me right? Do you know?" Oscar continued. Will didn't think it was funny.

"Your supposed to be an experienced bassist, that's what we need." Will said, he was sure of his playing technique.

"Listen when I play you wont believe it." Oscar said.

"Wrong, I write the music asshole, I ain't no Mexican director."

"Then stop thinking about it and play some, Bill." Oscar said.

"All right. Get out." Will said calmly.

"No." Leda interjected, "Let's hear him play." Holding true to her aura she calmed the situation down. Randy got up and went to the drums. Oscar took out his bass and Leda grabbed the microphone and leaned up against the couch where Oscar was sitting. She smiled at him and then Will counted them out.

They played an old song which Oscar recognized from the demo. At first he didn't play and then Oscar broke in putting his ideas into the strings. I do not know, his hard driving bass, gave the music an edge it didn't have before, something they had been looking for. He followed the changes perfectly. It worked, and it was different than Will had ever imagined. Oscar seemed just to not care about the music and do things simply in spite of Will. It simply and strangely complimented/completed Leda and the Swans. The song went on for more than ten minutes, they were having fun and when it was all over they all knew we had something special. They practiced all fourteen of Will's songs for the next three hours, it worked. Leda who was quite satisfied with Oscar; eventually it was said, "Okay, your in the band. We split everything evenly that has to do with the band and you can start tonight, at the Dragonfly. We got a deal?" We put out our hand

to shake his, Oscar looked her in the eye and asked, "When should I come over?"

"Around six." she answered and they shook hands. He leaned over and kissed her

on the cheek and Leda in spite of herself got a small chill and stuck her tongue ever so

slightly out at him. "See you guys then." Oscar said and started to pack his bass. "Wait."

Leda said, "What's your last name? You know, for the playbill."

"It's Oscar Oscar." he said and left.

"What a fucking idiot." Will felt when he was gone.

"What? You don't like him?" Leda asked "Should we start up?".

"I don't know, but I think we should call him Oscar the Grinch. He just takes."

Will joked.

"I don't see that" said Leda.

"Yeah, and we could put a picture of him in his trashcan next to his name on the

flyer. Oscar Oscar It'll be classic." Randy added.

"Do it." Leda said, "Print them up and I'll get them out around the city."

Downstairs, when Oscar got to the curb, a bum came up to him and started

rambling, "When all the money turns red and you hold it in your hands and it's

meaningless and all the people run in the street wondering who,; are you, and what they

are doing, it'll be the end of the world. The end of the world is coming, now."

"Get away from me you crazy son of a bitch. It is I." Oscar answered pushing

him out of his face. The bum looked at him with icy blue eyes, "Hey man you got a

dollar?"

"Kiss my boots." Oscar replied and walked away.

At six he returned to the loft. Will and Randy were packing a powder blue, newer model VW van with equipment.

"Where's Leda?" Oscar asked.

"Passing out flyers, she's coming." they answered. The same bum walked up as Leda was coming up.

"We know,; it's the end of the world." Leda said in a whiny tone and the bum looked at her eyes bulging. He stopped in front of Oscar and then in steps, like a sloth he slowly bent down onto his hands and knees and kissed Oscar's boots, "it's the end of the world". Bewildered they all looked at each other. Oscar began to laugh and kicked up knocking the homeless man on to his butt. He sharply stared at Oscar, "You got a dollar?" he asked. Oscar was about to spit on the man when Will stopped him and took out some change from his pockets and helped the bum up. Feed the hungry.

"Here, take this and get out of here...before he kills you." Will said and the bum took the money and began to leave.

"Yeah, and I don't ever want to see you around here again." Oscar continued. The bum began to jog away. He jogged all the way to the liquor store where he bought the little bit of beer he could afford. It was a strange scene. The swans never seen better.

"I just have that power over people." Oscar said laughing, then he noticed the playbill on the floor of the van, "And introducing bassist Oscar Oscar the Grouch" with a picture of the puppet in his trashcan home. He wondered if they know. They all started laughing and Will gave Oscar a little push. Oscar said Okay, and went upstairs to finish off getting the equipment.

When they got to the club they settled in and had some drinks, Will was busy setting things up. They were going on third that night.

Leda and Oscar began talking and hit it off. It made them both happy, Leda who naturally glowed lost some of her shine as the conversation continued. To Oscar she was becoming more human, but Leda was realizing she could be more serious with him. Was he him?

They rocked the crowd that night. People were cheering and dancing. Even the people at the bar were taking notice. The bass, guitar , drums and her voice was mockingly clear and transcendent. The sound was right. After the show they were all excited and happy, they decided to get more drinks.

At the bar Oscar was bombarded by women and he, the ham that he was, played it. Leda got more and more jealous and then found a friend of her own and began smoozing it. When Oscar looked over at her the guy she was talking to whispered in her ear and they began laughing. She kissed him on the cheek looking at Oscar. Oscar was furious and his neck turned a bright red. He put his arms around the girls he was liking, should I write talking to,? Will was sipping his whiskey sour and watching the show, Randy turned to him and asked, "How's it going?"

Will happy, was preparing himself incase Oscar was going to start a bar fight kinda thinking yes I, "He doesn't know it..." he said taking another sip of his drink, "but they're in doing love."

"Oh, cool. They completely I don't know the I." Randy said, taking a sip of his

bourbon and looking at <u>Leda</u>.

www.ingramcontent.com/pod-product-compliance
Lightning Source LLC
Chambersburg PA
CBHW030912180526
45163CB00004B/1805